FALLINGWATER

Edited by Lynda Waggoner
Photographed by Christopher Little

With essays by
Rick Darke, David G. De Long, Justin Gunther, Neil Levine,
John M. Reynolds, and Robert Silman

FALLINGWATER

In Association with the Western Pennsylvania Conservancy

RIZZOLI
NEW YORK

New York · Paris · London · Milan

The publication of this volume was made possible in part through the generous support of our sponsor

Colcom Foundation

to whom we extend our sincere gratitude.

First published in the United States of America in 2011 by
RIZZOLI INTERNATIONAL PUBLICATIONS, INC.
300 Park Avenue South, New York, NY 10010
www.rizzoliusa.com

ISBN: 978-0-8478-4847-8

Library of Congress Control Number: 2015955311

The essays by Edgar Kaufmann Sr., Liliane Kaufmann, and Edgar Kaufmann jr. included in the appendix (pp. 304-315) were first published, in slightly different form, in the Museum of Modern Art publication *The Show to End All Shows: Frank Lloyd Wright and The Museum of Modern Art, 1940* (Reed, Peter and William Kaizen, eds. Studies in Modern Art, no. 8. New York: The Museum of Modern Art, 2004), and are reprinted courtesy of the Museum of Modern Art, New York, and the Western Pennsylvania Conservancy.

Fallingwater is a property owned and operated by the Western Pennsylvania Conservancy. Fallingwater ® is a trademark and a registered service mark of the Western Pennsylvania Conservancy, with whom Rizzoli International Publications has collaborated in the creation of this volume.

Published on the occasion of the 75th Anniversary of the construction of Fallingwater, the celebration of which was marked by the Western Pennsylvania Conservancy throughout 2011.

Frank Lloyd Wright drawings © 2011 The Frank Lloyd Wright Foundation, Scottsdale, AZ.

Front endpapers: Though the region is characterized by forest, agriculture has long been part of the cultural landscape of the Laurel Highlands and the Allegheny mountain region of western Pennsylvania. Though far less varied in topography, Wright's native Wisconsin landscape was also a mix of forests, meadows, and farms. *Photograph by Rick Darke.*

pages 6–7: Perspective view of Fallingwater, pencil and color pencil on tracing paper, 33 x 17 inches, *The Frank Lloyd Wright Foundation FLLW FDN # 3602.004*

Back endpapers: January view from Route 381 just south of Fallingwater. The architecture of the primarily deciduous forest of the Laurel Highlands region is easiest to read when branches are bare in winter. The forest's larger patterns reveal the rolling topography of the region, which includes Pennsylvania's highest mountains. *Photograph by Rick Darke.*

Designed by Takaaki Matsumoto, Matsumoto Incorporated, New York

Distributed to the U. S. Trade by Random House, New York

Printed in Hong Kong

2021 2022 2023 / 10 9 8 7 6

CONTENTS

WESTERN PENNSYLVANIA CONSERVANCY

INTRODUCTION

By Lynda Waggoner

There is no place where Wright's architecture can be felt so warmly or appreciated so intuitively.
—Edgar Kaufmann jr.

Frank Lloyd Wright is arguably the most celebrated architect in American history and Fallingwater his most recognized example of the union of architecture and nature. Each year tens of thousands of visitors from the world over come to see and experience Frank Lloyd Wright's house over the waterfall, and it does not disappoint.

With a career that spanned nearly seventy years, Wright's contributions to modern architectural design are legendary: from the Robie House, his most developed manifestation of the Prairie Style, to the expressive sensuality of the Solomon R. Guggenheim Museum, the first museum to declare that the architecture was as important as the art inside. Wright created enduring precedents for the modern suburban house, office building, place of worship, and museum. However, Fallingwater has no progeny; it is a singular work that appeared almost without warning, its legacy difficult to define.

Fallingwater was born in 1935, thanks to a fortuitous convergence of people and circumstances. Wright was sixty-seven years old. He had begun his practice in 1894, had designed hundreds of buildings, and had secured an international reputation. However, by the mid 1920s his career was in decline. When the Depression arrived at the end of 1929, Wright found himself with few commissions and facing financial bankruptcy. In an effort to rebuild his reputation he embarked on a campaign to turn things around. He founded the Taliesin Fellowship, an outgrowth of an earlier apprentice program in which he paid young, aspiring architects a modest stipend in return for their having the privilege of working under the direction of a master. In this new incarnation he had the apprentices paying him to learn both architecture and his tenets of living. Housed at Taliesin, his home in Wisconsin, it would attract students from around the world. One of these students was Edgar Kaufmann jr., the only child of Edgar and Liliane Kaufmann, owners of a Pittsburgh department store.

The young Kaufmann was twenty-five in 1934 when he introduced Frank Lloyd Wright to his parents. The commission for a weekend house on property they owned in the mountains of southwestern Pennsylvania soon followed. Edgar Kaufmann Sr. was by all accounts a dynamic and charming personality who transformed his family's business into one of the nation's leading department stores. Despite the challenges of the Great Depression he had a ready supply of cash, and enjoyed turning architectural dreams into realities. It was the perfect union: a great architect desperately in need of reestablishing his reputation and a visionary client with deep pockets and an extraordinary site.

When the plans for the house arrived the family was surprised by its location over the waterfall rather than with a view of it. Nevertheless, they accepted Wright's plan almost without alteration. The materials chosen were sandstone from a quarry on the site to be laid up in an uneven horizontal fashion suggesting the way the stone appears in nature, reinforced concrete for the three cantilevered floor slabs painted a pale ocher color evoking its origins in the earth, walnut for the furniture and cabinetry, and steel for the window and door sash. Rising above the waterfall three

broad horizontal trays of reinforced concrete with upturned edges (parapets) define the floors of the main house. Stacked one upon the other they are separated only by long horizontal bands of windows. Almost half of each floor is outdoor space in the form of terraces. Anchoring the composition is a massive stone chimney from which the horizontal cantilevered floors extend to the west, and to the south reaching over the waterfall.

Nothing quite prepares us for seeing Fallingwater for the first time. Rounding a corner in the drive, there it is, what the artist Robert Irwin described as the "Aha!" moment. You see not the daring Fallingwater of photos but a modernist villa, its lines and planar surfaces an abstraction that, stepping down the hillside, seems to reveal the hidden structure of the hill itself. As you begin to move around it, you soon realize there is no front, no particular place from which the house is meant to be viewed. It is different from other buildings. Fallingwater reveals itself slowly. Each elevation suggests another aspect of its multifaceted character: daring yet sheltering, dramatic yet calm. It affects us both intellectually and viscerally; an extraordinary experience that both Edgar Kaufmann jr. and his father knew must one day be shared.

That happened in 1963 when the house and 1,600 acres were given to the Western Pennsylvania Conservancy by Edgar Kaufmann jr. He entrusted the organization not only with the care of one of Frank Lloyd Wright's great masterworks and an exceptional landscape but also with perpetuating the spirit of the place. In what was one of the greatest acts of philanthropy of all time, Kaufmann said, "The union of powerful art and powerful nature into something beyond the sum of their separate powers deserves to be kept living."

From the very start Fallingwater exceeded expectations. At the dedication ceremony one speaker speculated that perhaps someday as many as 25,000 visitors a year may find their way to its remote mountain location. The first year it was open to the public 30,000 people came. Today it attracts over 150,000 visitors annually from around the globe; it is a phenomenon.

For over forty years I have observed and participated in Fallingwater's evolution as a public site. I first came in 1965, a high school student seeking a summer job. I continued to work intermittently at Fallingwater while in college. Following graduation I held curatorial and administrative positions elsewhere for ten years, then returned in 1986 to become its first curator. In 1996 I was named director. I oversaw the first comprehensive documentation and conservation of its collections, the strengthening of its failing cantilevers, the restoration of the building, and the design and implementation of a landscape master plan. However, the most challenging task has been the preservation of the spirit of the place.

The success of a public site like Fallingwater is often measured by numbers: number of visitors, number of educational programs, number of publications, number of hits on its Web site, and sales at its museum store. As these numbers grow they impose new demands on the site: a need for increased professionalism, more staff, more policies, and more services. But sometimes, in the process of growing, one loses sight of the reason for being. Fortunately for us in the last years of his life Edgar Kaufmann jr. set out in writing and interviews his thoughts and beliefs about how Fallingwater and its program should evolve. He said, "Fallingwater is not an institution, it is a humane experience." From the beginning he focused on the visitor experience, something many museums have only paid attention to in recent years. He worried that, unless we were vigilant, much of what makes the experience of the site so exceptional could easily slip away without our even noticing.

In 1985 the conservancy commissioned an assessment of Fallingwater's operation by a highly regarded museum professional. In her report she called for stronger means of protecting the collections from visitors, suggesting that barriers between the visitors and the collections were in order; explanatory labels were recommended as was more scholarly information in the tours. Kaufmann wrote a five-page response that included this statement: "Wright's accomplishment as we came to know it intimately was rooted in a comprehensive insight into the quality of human existence, so comprehensive that the specialized routines of such agencies [preservation organizations, museums, and universities] would inevitably betray the value of Fallingwater, however productive they might be in different situations." He insisted visitors be permitted to walk into the rooms and not be cordoned off by velvet ropes. He asked that we strive to "make Fallingwater feel like a home, not a museum." He continued, "The art and objects should be treated decently and listed adequately, but always be in full subordination to the real values present," concluding with, "I would rather see a dozen articles broken or stolen each year than infringe on the real character of a visit to Fallingwater as established by the Conservancy." He wanted as little signage as possible throughout the site and certainly no labels inside the house. He disliked tours that are "dunked in expertise," preferring to keep them "simple, human and informal." He asked that there be no orientation film for visitors or even a model of Fallingwater at the visitor center, because he wanted the experience of seeing the house for the first time to remain fresh, its power undiminished.

This was a challenging and unorthodox mandate that I as the curator had some difficulty digesting. As I worked with Mr. Kaufmann and got to know the collections better, I slowly came to realize the wisdom of his approach. It was brought home to me one day when, while documenting the collections, I discovered that an important Tiffany vase had been broken and awkwardly repaired. Mr. Kaufmann had complained often about the housekeeping staff at Fallingwater and I could only think that they were the culprits. I sent the vase off for conservation and held a workshop for the staff on handling the collections and the need to report damage rather than repair it themselves. During my next visit to see Mr. Kaufmann I reported the accident, apologized, and discussed the measures I had instituted with the staff, hoping to avoid such incidents in the future. I concluded by assuring him that we had had the vase conserved and the damage was almost invisible. He smiled at me and said, "Lynda, don't blame the staff. I broke that vase and I glued it back together. You don't understand: Fallingwater was our weekend house. This is where all of the things that were damaged but too good to throw away ended up." As we worked our way through the collections it was clear that indeed this was the case. More important, I learned that Fallingwater is enlivened by its collections but not defined by them.

Edgar Kaufmann jr. was a leading scholar of architecture and design. A quiet man with a gentle manner, he could be utterly unyielding in his position when it came to Fallingwater. A series of prominent florists and interior decorators, engaged by the conservancy in an effort to make Fallingwater seem more homelike, left one after the other, wilted by his harsh reviews of their attempts. But he could also be charming and thoughtful. To celebrate his seventy-fifth birthday he brought elegant gifts for Fallingwater's administrator and director, remarking that he found it more satisfying to celebrate by giving presents to others than by receiving them himself.

Edgar Kaufmann jr. understood Fallingwater like no one else. Once asked what word best describes the house, he paused for a moment and responded, "Romance." He could not have been more right. If the goal of the Romantics entailed a return to nature, a belief in the goodness of humanity, and an exaltation of the senses then Fallingwater stands as a singular example of modern architecture that is romantic.

Fallingwater now celebrates its seventy-fifth anniversary. I have been asked: why another book? Hasn't it all been said; what is new; what more can be shown? These are good questions. Edgar Kaufmann jr.'s *Fallingwater: A Frank Lloyd Wright Country House* remains the most personal memoir of the circumstances surrounding the creation of the house and the life that was lived within it. Donald Hoffmann's *Frank Lloyd Wright's Fallingwater: The House and Its History* is likely the most accurate account of its history. Works by Franklin Toker, Robert McCarter, and others have added significantly to our understanding. However, there is still much to be learned.

Neil Levine has written extensively on Wright. His book *The Architecture of Frank Lloyd Wright* remains the standard for any study of the architect or his work. In his essay "To Hear Fallingwater Is to See It in Time" Levine deepens our understanding of Fallingwater as a place that, like nature itself, is ever changing, as he examines its relationship with our senses, the natural world, and time.

The garden as a place where nature is tamed to become at once beautiful and benign has always had a subtext: nature as dangerous. At Fallingwater these two competing ideas provide a contrast that enriches our experience of place. Here the architecture functions as both an invitation to nature and a protection from its wildness. Fallingwater becomes a safe sanctuary where nature's forces are kept at bay. Rick Darke has written extensively on the woodland garden. In his essay he examines Fallingwater's rich landscape and how it intersects with the architecture.

Fallingwater the house has always, and rightly so, overshadowed its collections. Nonetheless, the collections tell us much about the Kaufmann family and how they lived at Fallingwater. Justin Gunther, curator of Buildings and Collections, discusses the Kaufmanns' connoisseurship and how their choices inform our understanding of life at Fallingwater.

 Drawing on a recently acquired collection of over one thousand letters, David De Long clarifies some of the questions that have surrounded the younger Kaufmann's life in his article, "Kaufmann Family Letters: Edgar Kaufmann jr., Frank Lloyd Wright, and Fallingwater." De Long sheds new light on the man and confirms his role in connecting his father with Wright.

In 1995 I received a call from John Paul Huguley, a young engineering student who for his senior thesis was creating a computer model of Fallingwater's structural systems in an effort to better understand how the building worked. He reported alarming results: based on his analysis, Fallingwater was in danger of collapse. Panicked, I contacted our preservation consultants with the concerns and they responded, "We've seen nothing to suggest there's a problem. Elephants could dance on those terraces and they would still be fine." I decided we needed a second opinion. Robert Silman whose firm was engaged to strengthen the house explains in his article what the issues were and the techniques they employed to address them.

Fallingwater's legacy has always been a question of interest. When the architect Philip Johnson was at Fallingwater to celebrate his eighty-fifth birthday, he stood on its west terrace gazing at the tower window and declared, "It is the greatest house of the twentieth century." When we asked if we could quote him, he responded, "Certainly not. I've design a few buildings myself, you know." But Johnson was not alone in his assessment. Architects regularly vote Fallingwater as their favorite building. Given the affection for it, it is surprising that its impact hasn't been more evident in the work of the generations of architects who followed. Were the lessons of Fallingwater too difficult to assimilate? Was such a unique, site-specific building impossible to mimic? Or could it be that Fallingwater was born prematurely, that it has more to say to us today as we begin to examine more closely our relationship with our environment and the natural world? John Reynolds explores Fallingwater and its enduring legacy in his essay "Fallingwater: Integrated Architecture's Modern Legacy and Sustainable Prospect."

For seventy-five years Fallingwater has grown, and it continues to grow. Edgar Kaufmann jr. saw Fallingwater not only as an irreplaceable document of American art and values but also as a humane experience, where Wright's insight, the family's way of life, and the natural setting are spread out for all to experience and question regardless of their background or previous knowledge. Preserving the house and site for present and future generations is the primary mission of the Western Pennsylvania Conservancy's work at Fallingwater. Thanks to the guidance of wonderful teachers, we have strived to preserve the building and its site and keep the Fallingwater experience fresh and vital. Personally, I am indebted to Edgar Kaufmann jr., but also to Thomas Schmidt, Fallingwater's first director whose passion for the site is undiminished, and to a committee of thoughtful advisors who have never failed to tell me exactly what they think. But most of all, I am indebted to an exceptional staff, who have demonstrated through their patience and perseverance how deeply they care for Fallingwater and all it represents.

VISITING FALLINGWATER
THE DIRECTOR'S TOUR

By Lynda Waggoner

Fallingwater is a great blessing—one of the great blessings to be experienced here on earth, I think nothing yet ever equaled the coordination, sympathetic expression of the great principle of repose where forest and stream and rock and all the elements of structure are combined so quietly that really you listen not to any noise whatsoever although the music of the stream is there. But you listen to Fallingwater the way you listen to the quiet of the country…

—Frank Lloyd Wright, from a talk to the Taliesin Fellowship, May 1, 1955

For over thirty years I have been fortunate to have the opportunity to share Fallingwater with visitors from around the world. For me the chance to experience the house in every season, time of day, and weather condition has resulted in an even deeper appreciation for Frank Lloyd Wright's extraordinary achievement. While there is no substitute for experiencing Fallingwater first hand, I am pleased to share some of the unique features of this celebrated work in the following photographic tour.

page 18: Bird's-eye view of the southeast elevation showing the entire complex including the guesthouse at top. *right:* Plan of Fallingwater showing main house on Bear Run and Guest House. © *Astorino*

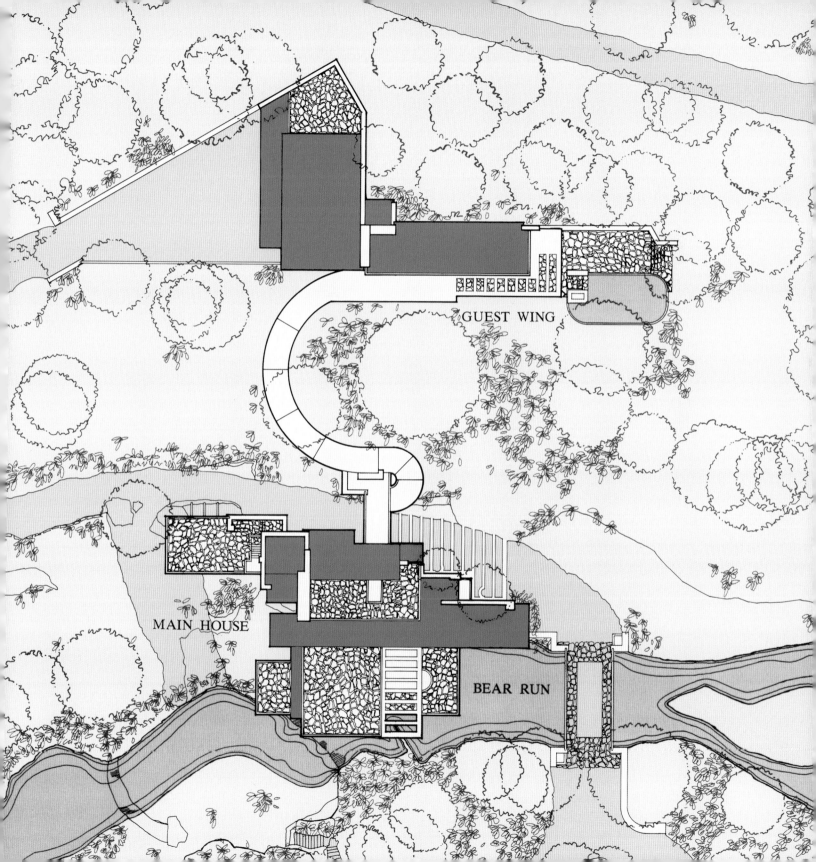

GUEST WING

MAIN HOUSE

BEAR RUN

Descending into the narrow valley created by Bear Run we slow and become aware of the smells, sounds, and richly textured character of the surrounding landscape. Remnants of the Kaufmanns' life at Fallingwater appear: cutting gardens hide the former gardener's cottage, and an old apple orchard marks the burial place of the family's 5 long-haired dachshunds.

As we round the bend of the driveway, an access road that existed before Fallingwater, the house begins to take shape through the trees. At first it is difficult to understand what we're seeing: is this the front, back, or side of the house? Then it appears—not the famous Fallingwater of so many photographs soaring over a waterfall, but a quieter Fallingwater hugging the side of the hill as it cascades down to meet Bear Run.

The reinforced concrete bridge introduces
us to the materials and forms of Fallingwater.
Anchoring the span are roughly laid stone
walls, which extend into the landscape on
each end. Built-in stone planters offer a
suggestion of domestication in an otherwise
wild landscape. The smooth surface of the
reinforced concrete provides a rich contrast
to the irregularity of the stonework. Wright
initially suggested the concrete be covered
in gold leaf. Ultimately, a warm ochre color
was chosen to compliment the cool gray of
the stone. The rounded parapets emphasize
the plastic nature of concrete.

The center of the bridge is defined by
a rectangular concrete slab, its corners
marked by four square lights under glass.
Flagstone pavers surround the slab and
introduce the flagstone floors of the
house beyond.

From the bridge the view of Fallingwater
is striking, as the house seems to hover
cantilevered over the stream.

A set of stairs hangs suspended from the
first floor just above the precipice of
the waterfall, which drops away behind it.
Wright considered blasting the streambed
at the foot of the stairs to create a pool
for swimming, but was advised against
it because the ledge of the waterfall
might have been destroyed in the process.
Instead, a four-foot-deep plunge pool
was added. It is entered from the terrace
by stairs concealed behind the massive
stone wall.

Upstream the water of Bear Run ripples over the bed rock that forms the ledge upon which Fallingwater sits. A rock face of Pottsville sandstone looms above. Its uneven horizontal layering inspired the masonry of the house.

View from upstream looking beneath
bridge toward house and falls.

Viewing the house from the east we are
reminded of a tree by the massive masonry
of the vertical walls—a trunk that anchors
the house to the ground. In contrast,
horizontal concrete planes thrust out like
branches on either side of the building.

Trellis beams stretch across the driveway
visually connecting the house to the
hillside above. The trellis also acts as
a rudimentary porte-cochère, signaling
where guests should be dropped off.
On the north side of the house, masonry
walls step back into the distance echoing
the forms of the rock face opposite them.
The stepping or layering of walls is a motif
that will be repeated throughout the
house. As with most of Wright's houses
we do not enter Fallingwater directly;
there is no front door. In fact, it is
difficult to locate the entry—a cave-like
slit between two walls.

About to enter, we notice the sound of the
waterfall is subsumed by the softer more
immediate sound of water splashing nearby.
Seeing a spout of water projecting out of
the wall and falling into a footbath below,
we are reminded of the importance of
water to this place. Used for washing after
a swim or a walk in the woods, it was also
where fresh flowers were left until they
could be arranged for the house.

Turning to the left, we rise up three steps
to the living room's east terrace and notice
the play of light on the stairs leading to
the covered terrace above. Suspended
from the wall and ceiling,
the stairs echo those that connect to
the stream.

left: Slipped between two stone walls we find the entry.

right: The foyer is small and confining with stone on three sides. There is room for only a desk and coatroom.

pages 48–49: From the foyer we are turned to the left, and ascending three steps we enter the living room from its corner. The space before us seems to open out in all directions, but we are drawn to the corner diagonally opposite where, in contrast to the cave-like entry, a sunny open terrace is visible. Once in the living room, we are surprised by the low ceilings. The polished stone floor suggests the wet stone of the streambed outside. Looking around, we are surrounded by built-in wood cabinetry, bookcases, a desk and long low seating suspended from the walls and a great stone fireplace. The central space is defined by a large square recessed light that is gently fitted into the ceiling. The effect is one of luxury but not extravagance. It is a place fitted to the purposes for which it was designed: reading, conversation, rest, and relaxation.

pages 50–51: On three sides there are long bands of windows occasionally interrupted by double doors that open out to terraces. Edgar Kaufmann jr. said the windows in Fallingwater so communicate what is happening in nature outside that they act like Japanese screens, which are changed with seasons. The steel window frames are all painted Wright's signature Cherokee Red, a color he used for all the metal in Fallingwater. He asserted that red best expresses the nature of steel: a product of red iron ore and fire.

pages 52–53: The functions within the room's open plan become apparent, with areas for music, study, conversation, and dining.

right: The compact music area is snuggly fitted into a recess in the stone wall. Lacking any window, its tight geometry includes high backed seating connected to a built-in hi-fi cabinet with shelves extending out and into the wall on the left. Wright used indirect florescent tube lighting throughout the house. Here it is concealed behind a wood panel dramatically lighting the stone wall.

left: From the second-floor covered terrace, we look down on one of the most complex moments in the house where inside and out are brought together. The semi circular stairwell leads to the stream below (the circle is a motif we will see repeated throughout Fallingwater). Only the well's curved end is open to the outside. Above, a trellis with skylights protects the interior but as it transitions to the exterior, it is unglazed and remains open. The stairwell and trellis beautifully express Wright's goal at Fallingwater "to bring the outside world into the house and let the inside of the house go outside" (*Frank Lloyd Wright, An Autobiography.* New York: Horizon, 1977, p. 166).

right: Beyond the desk the covering of the "hatch," like that of a ship, slides back to be concealed beneath a flower box. Two small doors open revealing the stairs, which we saw from the bridge earlier, and the stream below. The ceiling above opens to the sun through skylights. This penetration through the floor connecting it to water, and through the ceiling to the sky, is one of the most astonishing experiences in the house. The Kaufmanns questioned the functionality of the stairs but Wright claimed it was an essential element designed to "marry" the house to its site. It also helps to cool the living room in summer.

The living room's east terrace with stairs
connecting to the covered terrace above.

From this unusual vantage, we have a view of the bridge and Bear Run from the bottom steps of the staircase leading down from the hatch. At left is Jacques Lipchitz's *Mother and Child* on the wall of the plunge pool.

From the waters of Bear Run, we see the
hatch staircase, leading back to the living
room, and the edge of the falls beyond.

At dusk rooms seem to glow in
uninterrupted horizontal planes.

The terraces have a lightness about
them and on foggy days seem to float
in the mist.

left: The distinction between inside and
out becomes blurred as the interior stone
floor continues out to exterior terraces.
right: The tower window and the
chimney mass create the one strong
vertical element in this house noted for its
horizontal lines. From the small basement,
the windows continue uninterrupted
through third floor. Ceilings in the tower
rooms are beveled where they meet the
window so that the separation of floors is
not readily apparent from the exterior. At
night the furniture seems to float in space.

On the west terrace we experience a
sense of danger as we lean over the wall,
glimpsing the waterfall below. We feel
part of the falls and understand why
Wright placed Fallingwater above the
waterfall rather than on the hill opposite
with a view of the falls.

pages 72–73: The glass at the corners is mitered making the corners seem to disappear. Moving toward the terrace the sound of the waterfall becomes stronger. Wright-designed furniture surrounds us, with long expanses of integral seating, floor cushions, hassocks and coffee and end tables, all of which respond to the horizontality of the building's cantilevers.

left: Steel shelving visually pulls the disparate parts of the room together. Beginning on the left in the southern part of the room, it continues over the windows, where it also acts as mullions, curves around the fireplace, and finally terminates in a quarter circle at the stone wall in the north above the dining table (following page).

The fireplace is the focal point of the
living room. Its hearth, part of the natural
stone outcropping on which the chimney
is anchored, seems to erupt out of the
floor. The fire blazes in an opening that
is nearly six feet high. A great cast-iron
kettle, designed to hang from an arm
and swing out over the fire, was used for
mulling wine on cold winter days. When
not in use it fits neatly into a niche in the
wall created for it (previous page). To
the right of the fireplace is a food pass-
through from the kitchen to the dining
area. The light from the kitchen shines
through the door to the dining area;
however, this door was generally kept
closed. Elsie Henderson, the Kaufmann's
cook, recalled Mrs. Kaufmann rarely
darkened the threshold of the kitchen,
though Edgar Kaufmann Sr. frequently
came downstairs late at night looking for
the sandwich that was always kept waiting
for him in the refrigerator.

The kitchen window has one of the most spectacular views of the west terrace, suspended in space over the waterfall. The kitchen itself was designed by Wright to be essentially utilitarian in nature as the Kaufmanns had servants. The metal cabinets are by St. Charles; the Aga stove replaces an earlier one that was removed at the request of the family's cook, who found it too hot to work over in summer.

The dining area is located in the northern end of the living room. The walls here are comprised largely of stone and serve as a foil to the light and airy southern part of the room. Like all of the wood work in Fallingwater, the cabinetry is made of North Carolina walnut veneer over ship's quality plywood. The dining table can be extended by removing one or both of two drop-leaf tables set at the front of the buffet. Once removed, the table's leaves are raised and gate legs extended enabling the tables to be either free standing or attached to the end of the dining table, providing seating for nearly 18.

Tucked in the corner northeast of the dining area are the stairs leading to the second floor and guest house. At their foot hangs a portrait of Edgar Kaufmann Sr. by the artist Victor Hammer.

Having climbed the stairs, we look back over the curved opening of the stairwell, and see the possibilities beyond. To the left a distant light beckons at the end of a long dark hallway. In the center a separate set of stairs flanked by a stone wall on one side and bookshelves on the other offers the prospect of relaxation. On the right, a connecting bridge (unseen) invites us to explore the guest house on the hill above.

left: At the top of the stairs from the living room we come to the door to the guest terrace. Turning again we rise three steps as we did in the foyer downstairs, to reach the guestbath and bedroom (entry unseen).

right: There are four bedrooms in the main house, only one of which is a guest room. The bedroom seems small when compared to the living room. However, a guest house was planned from the beginning, though not designed until 1939 after the main house was completed. The room originally had a double bed as evidenced by the headboard. Every bedroom at Fallingwater has its own terrace and bath. The guest terrace, which is the only covered terrace, is accessible from the hallway outside the room or from exterior stairs of the first floor's east terrace. The guest bathroom also serves the living room.

The guest bedroom and terrace at dusk
as seen from the master bedroom terrace.

Entering the darkly lit hall we feel
constricted by the low ceilings and
narrow passageway and are drawn
to the light ahead.

Upon entering the master bedroom
we feel liberated by what seems a large
space after the confining experience of
the hallway. The fireplace is one of the
most dramatic in the house. Its opening
is counter-balanced by a niche created
by Wright specifically to hold the late-
Gothic sculpture of the Madonna and
Child. Shelves cantilevered from the
wall play upon the theme of ledge and
cantilever. On the right, the fireplace wall
is layered, stepping back in much the same
way as the wall along the drive below.

Wright designed wall-hung wardrobes
for the bedrooms. Edgar Kaufmann jr.
worked on some of the details including
the system of sliding shelves with caned
insets. In the master bedroom a full length
mirror is mounted on the inside of one of
the wardrobe doors.

The adjoining master bath used by Liliane
Kaufmann has a built-in vanity sink.
Geraniums in the window box planters
provide an element of privacy.

Edgar Kaufmann Sr. suggested the bathroom fixtures be hand hewn from native rock believing they would be more sympathetic to the goal of integrating nature into the building. However after receiving the cost estimates from local tombstone carvers and comparing those to commercial fixtures, he abandoned the idea. Ultimately, Kohler fixtures were selected in an ochre color similar to that of the concrete. He asked that the toilets be set low after having read of the health benefits of natural position toilets.

The master terrace is the largest in the house. Projecting out above the living room it offers three vistas: to the east we see the stream beyond the bridge; to the south a bank of rhododendrons; and to the west Bear Run forty feet below as it winds its way to the Youghiogheny River nearly a half-mile away.

A view from master bedroom terrace
looking west over the falls of Bear Run.

The south-east elevation reveals horizontal planes floating above Bear Run.

View of the central tower from the
master terrace.

pages 102–3: Edgar Kaufmann Sr.'s dressing room and study is a decidedly masculine space with stone walls on three sides and an imposing corner fireplace. A floor to ceiling window is notable for its lack of framing where the glass meets the stone. Instead, the glass is scribed and caulked directly into the stone, revealing a continuity of surface as the interior stone wall passes through the glass to exterior.

right: In the desk a quarter circle is cut out to allow the window to open. The motif is echoed in quarter circle wood shelves beside the bed.

Upon opening the corner casement windows, we are surprised to find no vertical support.

All of the bathrooms in Fallingwater,
including Edgar Kaufmann Sr.'s, pictured,
are lined in cork on the walls and floor.
A pleasant alternative to the cold, hard
stone, the cork was suggested by Edgar
Kaufmann jr. The horizontal sap lines
of the walnut veneer in the wall-hung
closet reinforce the horizontal theme
repeated throughout the house.

Located between the second and third floors, Edgar Kaufmann Sr.'s terrace is entered from the corner. From it we are presented multiple perspectives: on the left, the canopied walkway leading to the guest house, and, on the right, the master bedroom terrace and west terrace (unseen in photo). An expressive stepped concrete staircase reiterates the cascade theme and leads to Edgar Kaufmann jr.'s third floor study.

A view of Edgar Kaufmann Sr.'s terrace
from the staircase landing outside
Edgar Kaufmann jr.'s third floor study.

Located directly above his father's room,
Edgar Kaufmann jr.'s study shares the
same tower window treatment and desk
arrangement.

A reddish stone discovered in the same
on-site quarry that provided all of the
stone for Fallingwater is used here above
the shallow fireplace of Edgar Kaufmann
jr.'s study to great effect.

The desk of Edgar Kaufmann jr.'s study mirrors that of his father's study one floor below. In reviewing early plans for the desks, the Kaufmanns expressed concern that the radiator grills took up much of the writing surface. In what turned out to be a delightful solution to the problem, Wright extended the desks out past the adjacent windows, adding the quarter circle cut out to accommodate their opening.

Edgar Kaufmann jr. occupied
Fallingwater's third floor. This room was
originally intended to be his bedroom.
Instead, he added bookshelves and chose
to use it as a study. At right in foreground
is a bentwood lounge by Bruno Mathsson.
The chair's elegant, organic lines echo
the contours of the human form, creating
a design both beautiful and comfortable.

Off the study, a gallery extends more than twenty-six feet to the end of the third floor hallway. The hallway was originally intended to open onto a bridge, which would pass over the driveway, connecting the main house to a walkway leading to the guest house. However, it was decided that the bridge would be entered only from the second floor, leaving the hall on the third floor without a function. Edgar Kaufmann Sr. suggested it might provide a good location for a bed. Bright and sunny, Edgar jr. preferred it to the darker study initially designated to be his bedroom.

pages 124–5: Edgar Kaufmann jr.'s sleeping
alcove with a cleverly placed reading stand
that swings over or away from the bed.
left: Hallway from Edgar Kaufmann jr.'s
sleeping alcove leading to his study.

Detail of bookcase that lines the wall
of the interior staircase connecting the
second and third floors of the house.

Bookcase-lined staircase connecting
second and third floors of the house.

The bridge was added in 1939 to
connect the main house to the hillside
and walkway up to the guest house.
At its far end we see that a portion
of the cliff protrudes into the space.
Because Wright anticipated water might
seep from the hillside over the rock,
a trough was incorporated around its
base to drain the water outside.

On the right hand side of the bridge
leading toward the guest house a circular
stone moss garden continues through a
corner window to the exterior.

View from the walkway of the trellis
beams extending over the driveway below.

Covering the semicircular walkway, a
stepped canopy cascades down the hill
in folded planes suggesting the waterfall
below. Its drama is increased by the way it
seems to float in space supported only by
thin steel posts on the outside edge.

View of canopy from guest house toward
main house below.

left: Richmond Barthé's statue of Rose McClendon, positioned beside the canopy.
right: The canopy serves as a partial shelter for those passing between the main house below and the guest house above.

The guest house is at the top end of the canopy. Its entry is to the right, hidden by the projecting corner of the window.

A view from beneath the guest
house trellis.

The guest suite includes a sitting room
with a built-in bench that is deeper
than those of the main house and
often used as additional sleeping space,
especially for families with children.
The stonework in the guest house
is some of the finest at Fallingwater.
The corner fireplace incorporates
unusually large striated stones.

Shelves line the northern wall of the
sitting room and a continuous clerestory
window above opens to provide cross
ventilation. To the rear, a pocket door
slides into the wardrobe. When closed,
a glass panel allows the casework and band
of clerestory windows to continue into
the bedroom without interruption.

pages 150–1: The guest bedroom is modest in size, but double glass doors open out onto a terrace and swimming pool.

right: Like all of the bathrooms, the guest house bath includes a mirror designed by Edgar Kaufmann jr. A single panel of glass in a wood frame is mirrored in the center and frosted on the perimeter. Florescent tube lighting is concealed behind it.

The guest house terrace steps gracefully
down to the lawn. The overhang is
the longest cantilever at Fallingwater.
The overhang and wisteria covered
trellis provide shade for the guest house
in summer.

The corners of the guest pool are rounded.
Over six feet deep, its cantilevered stone
steps lead down into the water.

left: Screened by the massive stone chimney wall discreet stairs lead to servants quarters on the second floor of the guest house. Those on the left (not visible) go down to the basement laundry room.

right: To alleviate the need for the maids to carry buckets of water from one floor to the next, the Kaufmanns asked that a utility closet with a built-in cork sink be added at the top of the stairs on the third floor.

Servants quarters above the carport included three bedrooms and a walled terrace. A sitting room is on the left at ground level. The Kaufmanns were much loved by their staff. Although the project was dramatically over budget by the time the guest house was being finished, Mr. Kaufmann insisted these quarters be finished with the same high quality casework as the rest of the house.

The four-bay carport has a large courtyard with a long concrete wall used to screen the laundry's "drying yard" from the rest of the house. A clothes pole can be seen on the right. The driveway between the carport to the kitchen door at the main house functioned like the back staircase in the Victorian home. Using the driveway, servants could quietly perform their duties out of sight of the family and guests.

Returning to the main house by means
of the driveway, the integration of
house and site is evident in the powerful
anchoring of the bedroom terrace to
the rock outcropping.

162

While walking down the driveway,
back to the main house, we realize that
Fallingwater reveals itself slowly. Like a
sculpture it must be viewed from all sides
to be understood. There is no front or
back; every elevation shows us another
aspect of its nature.

The roaring falls beneath the house

in spring.

Leaving the house, we walk down a wooded path to the overlook for one last glimpse of Fallingwater. Suddenly, there it is—the famous view. The waterfall, which has only been hinted at until now, is in full sight. Seeing its massive ledge and cave beneath, we understand how these elements inspired the house with its cantilevered terraces separated by bands of dark windows. The power of the falls and the house together begin to wash over us. This is a fitting last impression: the culmination of all that we have experienced in the house. Pondering the scene, we realize that what we seek in art is the opportunity to connect with something deeper, more meaningful. In Fallingwater, Frank Lloyd Wright satisfied that need by giving us something we long for, the chance, at last, to be at home in nature.

KAUFMANN FAMILY LETTERS: EDGAR KAUFMANN JR., FRANK LLOYD WRIGHT, AND FALLINGWATER

By David G. De Long

In the fall of 2009, some two thousand letters and related papers concerning Edgar Kaufmann Sr. (1885–1955), his wife, Liliane (1889–1952), and their son, Edgar jr. (1910–89) (figs. 1–4), were sent to Fallingwater. Largely personal in nature, they had been kept by Edgar jr. and had never been made available for research. Upon Edgar jr.'s death, they came into the possession of his companion, the designer Paul Mayén (1918–2000), and upon Mayén's death, they were left to Mayén's nephew, Aldo Radoczy. Radoczy in turn gave them to Fallingwater, where they are now being catalogued. The following article, written to help commemorate the seventy-fifth anniversary of Fallingwater, is derived in the main from these letters, but can only suggest areas for future research once the archive is organized.

The earliest letters date from around 1927, when Edgar jr. was still at Shady Side Academy, the private school in the Pittsburgh suburb of Fox Chapel. He seems to have decided against continuing on to college; in one letter, his mother urges him to at least graduate from high school so that he could gain admission to college, should he one day change his mind.[1] In the end he did not change his mind about college, but instead moved to New York and into his own apartment. His father had his belongings shipped to him in December 1927 and wrote of being lonesome at home, reminding him that he was "only obligated for nine months with an option for the next twelve," advising him to "settle down and earnestly apply yourself to the work that you profess to love," and saying he "was charmed" after seeing the New York apartment.[2]

Presumably the work referred to was a loosely structured study of art under the direction of W. Frank Purdy, whom Edgar jr. later referred to as his tutor. In New York, Purdy was a director of the Ferargil Galleries at 37 East 57th Street and executive secretary of the Antique and Decorative Arts League, Inc., at 598 Madison Avenue, and he mentions first meeting Edgar jr. at the Ferargil Galleries in the months before.[3] He was later offered a teaching position as well as the chairmanship of the art department at the University of Kentucky, but declined.[4] The letters reveal Purdy—generally referred to as "Uncle Frank"—to be a close friend of the Kaufmanns and one to whom they offered both financial and personal support. But the letters give no hint as to how the connection was initially made. He may well have been consulted in their earlier art acquisitions, but of that I have found no definite proof. Liliane, hopeful that her son would one day go to Harvard or Yale, encouraged him to follow Purdy's advice regarding college at some later date.[5] With Edgar jr., Purdy clearly had a special bond, seeming to offer support that was otherwise lacking: "When I am with you, the confidence, the love, the faith, that are in you move me to tears— I am so desperately starved of them."[6]

By March 1929, following his period of unstructured apprenticeship, Edgar jr. had moved to Vienna, where he enrolled in the Kunstgewerbeschule, initially taking a course in drawing. Reflecting his aversion to formal schooling, he described it as "the place where all the best non-academic instructors are."[7] Used to luxurious accommodations, he rented a spacious studio for himself with breakfast and maid service included; apparently it lacked only a bathtub, which he had installed.[8] That summer, following a trip to Rome, he wrote his father that his work "was progressing steadily."[9] During holiday travels in May 1930, he wrote from Florence that "the most important event by far is that I went to call on Victor Hammer, with rather a dutiful sense about

174

fig. 1: Edgar Kaufmann jr. with his dog
(undated). *Western Pennsylvania Conservancy*

fig. 2: Liliane Kaufmann (undated).*Western Pennsylvania Conservancy.*

it, as you know I was never crazy about his work or even himself . . . . This time . . . we both got along marvelously . . . . I still don't consider his pictures masterpieces, [but] I think that his theories of painting are, on the whole, absolutely right . . . . I want to study with him."[10]

Austrian-born Victor Karl Hammer (1882–1967), who was earlier known to the Kaufmanns and who painted Edgar Sr.'s portrait in 1929, had apprenticed with architect and planner Camillo Sitte (1843–1903), then later studied at the Academy of Fine Arts in Vienna. He became known as a painter, sculptor, printer, and typographer, and from 1929 to 1934 maintained his studio in Florence at the Stamperia del Santuccio, where Edgar jr. had joined him by 1931.[11] A description of Hammer's studio seems to prefigure Frank Lloyd Wright's Taliesin Fellowship to which Edgar jr. would later be drawn: "Routine art school methods are excluded. Teaching would be done through work on actual commissions carried to completion."[12] Reinforcing this parallel, Edgar jr. later described the work there as producing "organic, living products."[13] He had rented his own apartment in Florence by March 1931, which his mother described as "much nicer than he had in Vienna."[14]

The family's connection with Hammer was somewhat complex. To support his work, they had established a foundation on his behalf in October 1928, and during his stay in Florence, Edgar jr. donated $600 of his monthly allowance to the enterprise, retaining $200 for himself.[15] In return, Edgar jr. believed that his father "owned everything produced by him and under his direction."[16] His father was supportive of the endeavor and of his son's diverse work there, mentioning "the printing shop, painting and sculpturing . . . the money to come from Mother and myself . . . . I am certainly proud of your being willing to contribute so much of your allowance for the continuance of the work in which you seem to be so engrossed."[17]

Showing confidence in his son's ability, Edgar Sr. commissioned him to design a new office at Kaufmann's department store in collaboration with Hammer; Edgar jr. later suggested that more credit should go to Hammer than himself, but in the end nothing seemed to have resulted.[18] Early in 1933, Edgar jr. accompanied Hammer to London, where he studied bookbinding under Douglas Cockerell and rented a studio of his own.[19] By then, during the Great Depression, Edgar jr. was becoming aware of money problems affecting his family. His father had earlier written, "As to the store—business has never been so bad."[20] His mother had written of their need to save money and of the possibility of having to move to a more economical apartment from their luxurious house, La Torelle (1924–25), which had been designed by the prominent Pittsburgh architect Benno Janssen (1874–1964) and built in the Pittsburgh suburb of Fox Chapel.[21] Later she wrote that wages had been cut at the store, that dividends were being diverted from their personal accounts, and that "Father will have very little income; we will simply have to revise our manner of living."[22] In 1933, just as Edgar jr. was settling in London, his father wrote, "We will end the year at a decline of about seven millions of dollars gross selling—the greatest decline in any of the 61 years of the business . . . the first year in history that we have actually lost large sums of money."[23] So whatever his concerns with the darkening situation in Germany, money issues also had to be on Edgar jr.'s mind. In February 1933, he gave six-months notice to Hammer, and in late July he returned to the United States.[24] He had already begun to register impatience with Hammer, writing his father, "Now I am convinced that Hammer's personality is what guarantees the stillbirth of his ideas."[25]

In 1936 Hammer moved to Vienna, then in 1939 moved on to the United States, later teaching at the University of Kentucky in Lexington. Paintings in possession of the Kaufmanns were offered as a gift to that university in 1961.[26]

During her son's last year in Europe, in spite of the Depression or perhaps because of it, Liliane made plans to open an exclusive boutique—to be known as the Vendôme shops—on the eleventh floor of Kaufmann's department store. The Kaufmanns had long been traveling extensively in Europe, partly to maintain contact with the store's representatives, and during their son's sojourn there to also visit him (fig 3).[27] Now they provided a buying opportunity for Liliane as well. She consulted with her son regarding the design of the shop and was proud of its success. Shortly after it opened in March 1933, she wrote to him, "I have never been so happy in my life as I am just now. I never dreamed that running a shop could be so interesting . . . . I find myself a very competent saleswoman."[28] She also worked extensively as a volunteer at Montefiore Hospital in Pittsburgh (fig. 5) and served as its president from 1934 to 1943.[29]

After his return from Europe, Edgar jr. seemed less focused. He may have lived for part of the time at La Torelle, and he almost certainly resumed close contact with Purdy. He later recalled that he settled in New York, feeling "disconnected from the thoughts and ways of America after long study in Europe."[30] In that same paragraph, he recounted how a friend recommended Frank Lloyd Wright's *An Autobiography*[31] and, reading it, "believed Wright saw what I was missing." This led him to join Frank Lloyd Wright's Taliesin Fellowship in 1934. He was indefinite as to the name of the friend, remembering only that it was a woman who worked as a secretary in an art gallery.[32] This gap in documented history has led to speculation by Franklin Toker in his exhaustively researched, informative history of Fallingwater.[33] Toker concluded that this woman was fictional and that Edgar jr. instead went to the fellowship as an emissary for his father (who was considering Wright for a number of Pittsburgh commissions), leading him to the sad conclusion that "it makes clear that Edgar [jr.] had no role whatsoever in designing Fallingwater."[34] The Kaufmann family letters indicate otherwise.

By his own admission, Toker explained that he had angered Edgar jr. with what were

fig. 4: Edgar Kaufmann jr. and Edgar Kaufmann Sr. (undated).

Western Pennsylvania Conservancy.

fig. 5: Liliane Kaufmann (undated). *Western Pennsylvania Conservancy.*

considered intemperate remarks given at a symposium in 1986 in honor of Edgar jr. at Columbia University, and as a result communication was terminated and further access to papers denied.[35] This may help explain Toker's often derogatory tone. His persistent reference to Edgar as "Junior" reflects this, for all who respected Edgar jr.'s wishes knew he hated to be so termed. Even the use of the upper case J in "Edgar Kaufmann Jr." provoked his irritation, especially following his father's death. As a reflection of his intense feeling in this regard, Edgar jr. once rejected an entire run of custom-embossed stationery for a not-for-profit organization (at their expense), insisting that it be reprinted with his name properly spelled.[36]

As the Kaufmann letters make clear, there was indeed a woman working for a New York gallery—the Ferargil Galleries—by the name of Edna Offner; she was mentioned several times in the correspondence and was much praised by Purdy.[37] In October 1934, she wrote to "Uncle Frank," "I was utterly amazed by the news about June's giving up his plans for that New York studio and going with Wright! I guess I started something when I wrote to you about the 'Autobiography.' It should be wonderful training for him, but I am terribly disappointed that he will not be with you."[38] Shortly after, she wrote to Edgar jr., "It was startling news to learn from Uncle Frank of your decision to study with Wright, and then so soon to find you established at Taliesin. What a glorious opportunity to live so close to the logic and wisdom of a man as courageous and free as Wright!"[39]

Edgar jr.'s time with the fellowship is well documented. He went to Taliesin for an interview in late September 1934 and joined the fellowship in mid October.[40] On October 20, his father wrote, "To-day is the seventh day of your departure . . . . Your letter sort of dazed me . . . . I can well understand that all in all you have found it fascinating and diversified . . . . I cannot tell you how really happy I am that you are there."[41] Purdy also voiced his support, writing that he agreed "with your present environment utterly."[42] Edgar jr. wrote his parents, "So far I continue to get more and more enthusiastic about Wright and Taliesin . . . . There are all the petty personal undercurrents one would expect in such a group, but they really seem to be relegated to their proper sphere."[43]

Shortly before Halloween that year, he encouraged his parents to visit, partly because he wanted to join them in Chicago so that he might buy warmer clothing.[44] In that same letter he added that he had been asked by Wright to read some of the translations from German he had made of Lao-Tze, and that Wright remained "increasingly inspiring." The Kaufmanns visited in late November, following which Liliane wrote to her son, "I was so happy about you—I saw so clearly (perhaps for the first time) what you wanted and how surely you would get it—I was so glad to have seen Taliesin with my eyes and felt it with my heart."[45]

As documented elsewhere, Wright met with Edgar Sr. in Pittsburgh in mid December 1934 to discuss various projects that he might design, including a planetarium and a new office for Kaufmann; they also visited Bear Run and initiated a discussion about a new weekend house. By then, Edgar Sr. had agreed to fund the building of the Broadacre City models, which were to be exhibited in New York the following year.[46]

In January 1935, the Taliesin Fellowship relocated temporarily to Chandler, Arizona, where quarters were provided for their work on the models.[47] Edgar jr. wrote of being settled in La Hacienda, "an ex-tourist camp, and as such quite adapted to our needs—tho not beautiful . . . . The model requires lots of work on everyone's part . . . . We work in the roofed patio."[48] As he was used to comfortable places of his own with great freedom to plan his own schedule, he began to chafe at the restricted options. Giving early indication of this and of his assumed role in the design of Fallingwater, his mother wrote, "I know what you are going thru—it's hell. But . . . don't stay because of the house. It will be built and your criticism will be just as valuable if not more so, away from there as there on the spot."[49]

When the Broadacre models were completed, Wright selected four apprentices to drive them to New York: Edgar Tafel and Robert Mosher driving a truck, with Robert Bishop and Edgar jr. following in the latter's convertible.[50] Once there, they organized the materials for the exhibition in anticipation of its scheduled opening (and Wright's arrival) on April 15, 1935. Following that, rather than continuing his apprenticeship, Edgar jr. returned to Pittsburgh, where he joined Kaufmann's staff, soon rising to the position of merchandise manager for the home department.[51] He had evidently forewarned his father, who wrote to him upon his arrival in New York, "I am just pulling at the traces to start moving the load and double harness with you."[52] Those remaining at Taliesin seemed unprepared for this turn of events. One apprentice, Bill Bernoudy, wrote, "Your precipitous departure cut me off from the opportunity of thanking you for the many privileges I enjoyed during our brief friendship. But I rather imagine that you find yourself now enjoying a more liberal measure of independence than one is able to at Taliesin."[53]

Edgar jr.'s six-month apprenticeship was not exceptionally short. Others had stayed for less time, some, it seems, even leaving after only a few days, frustrated by the restricted schedule and unexpected hardships that understandably affected Edgar jr. as well.[54] Yet gossip surrounding homosexual behavior at the fellowship may have precipitated the event.[55] A letter from apprentice Sim Richards suggests this might have been the case: "The whole affair was stupid and awfully tiresome for a number of us . . . . As a matter of fack' [sic], Mr. Wright spoke to me of it the day I last saw him in Arizona and I ups and told him just what I thought of you . . . that I had no evidence from you or anyone in the Fellowship—and by the way, I once made a typical Richards pun on that by spellin' it Phallus-ship . . . . I said that I thought that all the Gossip that whirls around here was a pretty sad thing . . . . He agreed."[56] In that same letter, Richards alluded to Wright's feelings about Edgar jr.: "He said he didn't think you were the sort of person we need around here and I said that I could name a handful here who didn't enter one tenth into the group life as you did—who were not nearly so thoughtful or willing."[57] Whatever the reasons, Edgar jr. remained loyal to Wright, becoming, in fact, one of his greatest defenders. In return, Wright in several instances showed special respect for him, as when he wrote Edgar Sr., "You have a fine son . . . . Give him a real share of responsibility. He will go down unless you give him now this trust in him by his sire . . . . I know he worships you at heart. I've seen him suffer."[58]

Again living in Pittsburgh, Edgar jr. was in an ideal position to contribute to the design and construction of Fallingwater. Its history—from first discussions in 1934 until its completion late in 1937, with a guest house to follow—has been much chronicled and need not be repeated here.

fig. 6   fig. 7

Most have accepted the fact that Edgar jr. helped supervise construction and served as intermediary between his father and Wright's office.[59] Few have questioned his modest claims that he contributed details that helped clarify its design. These included suggesting cork surfaces for the bathrooms, designing a system of cane-lined sliding trays for linens, and promoting the use of fluorescent tubes—then newly available—to help light the living area.[60] Correspondence among the letters donated by Edgar jr. to the Avery Library at Columbia University documents other involvements: his modification of furniture dimensions (which Wright approved)[61] and his authorization to proceed with cabinetwork. With one expensive and seemingly unnecessary element of Fallingwater he was forcefully involved: the suspended stairs leading from the glazed hatch in the living room to the falls below, seemingly stairs with no real function. When questioned, Wright had telegraphed that the "hatch has no meaning without intimate relation by stair to stream . . . . This feature [is] absolutely necessary from every standpoint."[62] Edgar jr. argued persuasively for its retention.[63] Perhaps equally important, Edgar jr. helped convince his mother of the rightness of Wright's concept and of the value of modern design. Earlier she had written, "Why is it so comfortable to sit in rooms with great high ceilings? I know they're not supposed to suit our modern way of living—but there you are—they suit me."[64] Visiting Fallingwater near the time of its completion, she had written that she liked the crane in the living room fireplace, but "the shelves still distress me. I changed the convector in my bath—took ½ of it only & furred it so that it fits into the cement return & leaves the glass shelf clean."[65] Writing from Buffalo, where he had gone to supervise details of Fallingwater's upholstery, Edgar jr. described visiting Darwin H. Martin's widow in her Wright-designed house (1903–06); Mrs. Martin, it seemed, had found her bedroom details "too masculine and ungraceful" but came to the understanding that as a woman she could learn to "soften and intimize [sic] them successfully and happily." Similarly, Liliane came to appreciate her own bedroom at Fallingwater.[66]

The Kaufmanns began to use the house in the fall of 1937 (figs. 6–7), and Aline Bernstein Louchheim (1914–72)—a distant cousin and family friend—praised its design to John McAndrew, who had been one of her teachers at Vassar and who was then the new curator of architecture at

fig. 8

the Museum of Modern Art in New York.[67] After visiting the house, McAndrew agreed that it was exceptional, and mounted a special exhibition at MoMA from January 25 to March 6, 1938. In preparation he had contacted Wright, who replied, "All right John let's see what you can do. Coffman [sic] Junior has best photographs I've seen of house."[68] The twenty-three panels mounted for the exhibition included nineteen photo panels, most by Pittsburgh photographer Luke Swank.[69] The exhibition itself led to Edgar jr.'s own involvement with MoMA, which only ended in 1955, as discussed below.[70]

In 1941, Edgar jr. rented an apartment in Mexico City so that he might devote more time to painting.[71] Fallingwater continued to provide a place of welcome respite for his parents. His mother wrote, "There must be something about close contact with nature which helps to heal everything"; and his father wrote, "It is still the one great haven and if it weren't for the several days a week there, I really doubt whether I could take it."[72] Around that time they decided to sell La Torelle and were looking for property in the Pittsburgh neighborhood of Mount Washington where they might build an apartment building into which they could move, an idea that Edgar jr. had earlier suggested; the eventual commission for the Point View Residence went to Frank Lloyd Wright in 1951.[73] At some point they closed Fallingwater for what must have been a relatively brief time, but reopened it in 1943, and Edgar Sr. vowed never to close it again, writing later that same year that Fallingwater was "both a great haven for retreat and pleasure."[74]

By the time Fallingwater was reopened, Edgar jr. was serving as a military intelligence officer with the 5th Army Air Force and primarily assigned to duty in New Guinea (fig. 8).[75] Describing his living conditions, he wrote, "I'm sitting in one end of our only screened building—a big . . . kitchen and dining hall . . . . Otherwise we live in big tents . . . scattered up and down a very steep and craggy green hillside, and we face a jungle wall, chaotic and unattractive."[76] Letters from home included several impassioned ones from Aline Bernstein Louchheim. In one she referred to their having slept together, and in another recounted, "I remember clearly asking you, irrelevantly, if you had ever wanted to sleep with me and your answer, 'Yes—but only out of curiosity.'"[77] That she was then married to Joseph H. Louchheim seems not to have impeded her show of affection.

fig. 8: Edgar Kaufmann jr. (left) with unidentified solder in New Guinea (undated). *Western Pennsylvania Conservancy.*

fig. 9 (right): Edgar Kaufmann jr., portrait by Donald Friend, 1944, Pen and ink, 25.7 x 17.4 cm (MS5959, item 27). *Courtesy National Library of Australia, Canberra.*

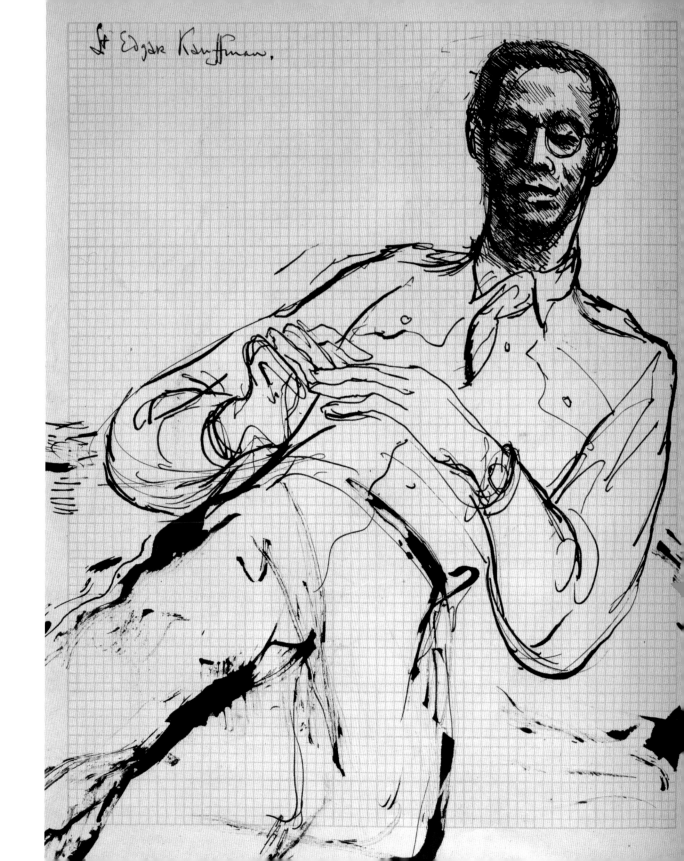

To Edgar Kauffman.

They were divorced in 1951, and she may well have imagined that her union with Edgar jr. would at last be formalized,[78] but that was not to be. Instead, she married famed American architect Eero Saarinen (1910–61) in 1954.

Military duty apparently left ample time for leave in Australia, where Edgar jr. met the renowned Australian artist Donald Friend (1915–89) and acquired two of his remarkable, richly illustrated diaries.[79] Friend sketched his portrait (fig. 9), to which Edgar jr. reacted, "The sensation of your new book [*Painter's Journal*] was my hips—all my friends really believe I looked like that, poor dears—Flatterer!"[80] Elsewhere Friend characterized Edgar with knowing perception; among several entries, he wrote, "He is a most extraordinarily charming and clever person" (July 15, 1944); "rather unpredictable" (August 2, 1944); "so bloody indirect and oriental in his approach, is so bound by outlandish American tribal codes, subtle, complex and incapable of saying directly what he wants or means" (September 9, 1944); "his observations of life are delightfully acute and humorous. He has that gift of observing and enjoying the moment whilst it is actually occurring, extracting from the present not only its own especial favour, but also adding to it the essence of past happenings to make it more complete" (October 12, 1944).

At the conclusion of the war, Edgar jr. returned not to Pittsburgh but to New York, where he resumed his affiliation with the Museum of Modern Art, serving as director of the Department of Industrial Design from 1946 to 1948 and as curator of the Good Design exhibitions from 1950 to 1955.[81] At the same time his parents were spending winters in Palm Springs, California, where they built another modernist icon: the Kaufmann House (1946) by Richard Neutra (1892–1970). Liliane had written, "I think Neutra is a great charmer and Mrs. N. is very refreshing and intelligent. . . . In case we really should build I hope you will help us on the plans."[82]

As other Kaufmann letters suggest, their marriage was not a happy one, and during several periods over the years they had lived separately. Things seemed to worsen in 1951, when Liliane decided to leave Fallingwater forever and build a house of her own—not in Palm Springs, but near Ohiopyle, Pennsylvania, where she found desirable property on Beaver Creek. She voiced regret at things she would always miss about Fallingwater: "the pink laurel at Lover's Leap, the white dogwood against the dark rock over the pool; the way the hillside looks when the Judas trees and the blue-bells and the pink dogwood all blossom together; places in the woods where lady's slipper grows in the spring . . . all these and many more are a part of me."[83] She asked Frank Lloyd Wright to design her new house, writing, "The house in Palm Springs will in no sense have anything to do with me. . . . Edgar and I will never again share a house. That also means that when he returns I must leave Fallingwater which is a great sorrow to me . . . . The great point is whether you would be willing to design and build the house for me—that is what I would like best."[84] Yet Wright did not respond, and she wrote a second letter asking if he had received the first, at the same time telling her son that she had offered the commission to Wright but had not had any response.[85] It seems inconceivable that Wright would have ignored her plea, yet her letters may never have been sent: there is no record of them in the index of Wright's correspondence,[86] and the letters in the Avery archive are the handwritten originals, with no sign of any postmark.

In the end Liliane returned to Fallingwater, yet during this time seemed far from happy; she wrote to her son, "I don't think I can possibly go on living."[87] In a short piece intended to be part of the Museum of Modern Art's catalogue accompanying their major exhibition of Wright's work in 1940, she had written of her own room as her favorite at Fallingwater: "I began to glory in the sense of space and peace with which my room filled me."[88] It was there she was found near death from an overdose—possibly accidental—of sedatives. A local doctor was summoned, and in a desperate attempt to save her she was rushed to Pittsburgh, but to no avail. She died on September 7, 1952.[89] By then Edgar Sr.'s health was declining. Two years later he married a woman by the name of Grace Stoops and spent increasing time in Palm Springs. Visiting him shortly before his own death in 1955, his son acknowledged Stoops's "good deed" in caring for him those last months, but remained unhappy with Neutra's design: "It's still a mess of a house. The garden is too paradisiacal for words . . . ."[90]

In the years that followed, Edgar jr. continued to publish scholarly works—especially on Wright—and for many years taught at Columbia University, where he held the rank of adjunct professor.[91] In 1963, in accordance with what he and his father had earlier discussed, he gave Fallingwater to the Western Pennsylvania Conservancy together with a modest endowment.[92] Yet it could not have been easy; he had explored ways to continue using the house, but was advised by his attorney that any such use would negate tax advantages.[93] He remained close to Olgivanna Lloyd Wright, Wright's widow (1897–1985), as many letters from her show; in 1984 she wrote, "You are my best beloved oldest friend on earth."[94]

In the mid 1970s, Edgar jr. acquired three attached houses on the Greek island of Hydra, combining them to form a summer retreat. He also fitted out a fishing boat with bunks and a dining table to accommodate luxurious lunches on a Greek sea. Recalling him at that time, Donald Friend wrote that he was one of the most important individuals in his own life: "Whenever these persons take up an abode there is a localized expansion of consciousness. Creativity is heightened, the life of those around them improves. They are in a sense 'culture heroes.' Ideas are born. Nothing is quite the same again. The processes are casual and unregulated, and have no end in view (nor profit) except a realization of the better possibilities of living. To which the arts are essential" (January 14, 1975). It is these very traits that reinforced Edgar jr.'s profound appreciation of Fallingwater. Only a few years before his own death, he praised Fallingwater as "a powerful statement of the fertile relationships between mankind and the natural environment . . . rooted in a comprehensive insight into the quality of human existence."[95]

TO HEAR FALLINGWATER IS TO SEE IT IN TIME

By Neil Levine

fig. 1

fig. 2

Frank Lloyd Wright's Fallingwater, the country house the architect designed for Edgar and Liliane Kaufmann in 1934–35 and built in 1936–37 in the Allegheny Mountains, is one of the most extraordinary and celebrated works of architecture of the twentieth century. It stands out as a singular expression of integrating a building with its natural environment and creating out of that a synergy that has become definitive of the modern concept of site-specificity. For those who have not seen it in reality, the house is known primarily through the canonical view from below the waterfalls the structure incorporates (fig. 3). This image, however, can be quite deceiving—and reductive. Not only is that view unavailable to first-time visitors arriving at the house in the usual way; it is also a view that is deliberately deferred until one has thoroughly experienced the house and takes the time to look back and meditate upon it. It thus only becomes truly meaningful as a fulfillment of the mounting perceptions and expectations that progressively lead to and inform it. This essay will describe this temporal process of discovery and, through it, try to explain the house in all its complexity.

Fallingwater is mysterious as a presence in the landscape—its imagery as evanescent, multivalent, and ambiguous as the various faces it presents to the observer. When seeing it from the access road for the first time, it is difficult to know precisely what one is looking at (fig. 1). Is it bands of mist rising up the glen through the forest? Or is it a mirage of natural terracing of the cliff face itself? From some vantage points the house looks to be fundamentally made of stone—heavy, earthbound, and one with the boulders in the streambed from which it emerges (fig. 2). From others, it looks to be entirely composed of concrete—light, pneumatic, hovering in space over the water (fig. 4). But is the stone just stone, or do its texture and verticality not remind us of the surrounding trees? And is the concrete merely concrete, or is it not assimilable to the white water (fig. 5)?

Once inside the house, one immediately relates the highly polished, waxed stone floor to the streambed over which it lies (fig. 12). On the terraces off the second- and third-floor bedrooms, one's thoughts turn from the water to the surrounding tree cover. The sensation is of being in a tree house (fig. 6), so much so that now one thinks of Fallingwater entirely in terms of the vegetation that surrounds and embraces what was referred to as the Kaufmanns' "forest lodge."[1] But in the

page 188: View from lawn before guest house in spring looking toward main house and bridge below.

fig. 1: View from access road. Photo by author.

fig. 2: Entrance at rear of house.

fig. 3 (right): View from below second falls.

fig. 4: View from bridge.

fig. 5: Falls beneath living room and terrace.

fig. 6

end, it is the waterfalls that define the house and are why Wright named the building after this most prominent of the site's natural features. And so we come back to the image where we started but with a much greater sense of the complexity of the issues it embodies as a cumulative one of the building.

MoMA's 1938 Exhibition Catalogue and the Recognition of Real Time and Virtual Time
Fallingwater, as its name implies, is about movement and change and the continuous effects and action of time. It incorporates these very phenomena in its forms. There is no one point of view, no privileged spot for the gaze to alight upon—no single moment in time that becomes the representative, pregnant one. In part, this is a function of the medium of architecture, which presents itself as a three-dimensional sequence of spaces to be traversed and experienced in time. Philip Johnson called this the "processional element in architecture."[2] But there is more to it than that, for Fallingwater exploits this normal characteristic of the medium to produce an architectural condition where time is understood not merely in the literal terms of one's movement through space in real time but also as a more profound sensation of the virtual time of duration.

That dual experience of time in Fallingwater was recognized, and highlighted, as soon as the building was completed, in the exhibition devoted to it by the Museum of Modern Art in New York in early 1938. For the museum's first major one-building exhibition, John McAndrew, the curator of Architecture and Industrial Art, produced a catalogue including plans, an explanatory text by the architect, and photographs of the structure taken mainly by Bill Hedrich, of Hedrich-Blessing, and Luke Swank, a family friend of the Kaufmanns.[3] The arrangement and layout of the photographs stress the temporal experience of the visitor in the perception of the house.

Beginning with the title page, the sequence of views starts at the bridge leading to the structure (fig. 7). Following the text by Wright and a double-page spread of plans, an extended series of two-page spreads leads the visitor around and through the building, focusing on its multiple aspects.[4] To illustrate the course of movement and allow the reader to follow it in his or her mind's eye, there is a diagrammatic plan beneath each photograph with a small eye drawn to indicate the

fig. 6: Third-floor terrace. _Photo by author._

A NEW HOUSE BY FRANK LLOYD WRIGHT

ON BEAR RUN
PENNSYLVANIA

THE MUSEUM OF MODERN ART · NEW YORK · 1938

fig. 7

fig. 8

physical point of view (fig. 8). These spreads are interrupted once, in the middle, by a pair of dramatically opposing views of the house, both by Luke Swank and both lacking the situational ocular index. More significantly, and much more unusually, the processional sequence culminates on the final page of the catalogue in a collage of two photographs, one above the other, both taken by Bill Hedrich and both showing the house from precisely the same point of view. The only difference is that the upper one was taken in the daytime and the lower one at night (fig. 9).[5]

The final two images go beyond an acknowledgement of the literal time it takes to see the house and reveal a sense of the building's durational aspect. The highly unusual juxtaposition of two views of the same building at different moments in the diurnal cycle leads one to contemplate the fact that Fallingwater is not only about one's passage through time but, even more importantly, about the passage of time itself, a virtual time made manifest in the building's synergistic presence in an ever-changing landscape. Such an effect is echoed in the continuous sound of the falling water, which brings to mind the interrelationship between seeing and hearing in the experience of Fallingwater and Wright's intention to bring the latter to bear on the former.

Listening and Hearing vs. Seeing and Looking

In the text explaining his design, Wright wrote that the house was conceived for someone "who liked to listen to the waterfall" and that it was consequently designed as a "living space over and above the stream."[6] No mention was made of the view, either of the falls or of the surrounding forest. The architect was even more explicit in the letter he wrote to his client following an initial site visit in late 1934. The purpose of the trip was to scout the approximately 1,600-acre property Kaufmann owned in southwestern Pennsylvania for the best location for the house. Kaufmann led his architect to the spot along Bear Run where the streambed drops precipitously down the high-walled glen to create a series of falls (fig. 10). This was a spot favored by the Kaufmanns for swimming, picnicking, sunbathing, and the like. Wright later recalled that his client pointed to the large boulder just to the left of the upper falls as the place where he liked to sit and enjoy the atmosphere. Apparently, both Wright and Kaufmann agreed that the new house would be located

fig. 7: Frontispiece and title page of catalogue of Museum of Modern Art 1938 one-building exhibition (*A New House by Frank Lloyd Wright on Bear Run, Pennsylvania*. New York, The Museum of Modern Art, 1938). *Courtesy of The Museum of Modern Art, New York. Photograph by Bill Hedrich. Chicago History Museum. HB-04414-Y2.*

fig. 8: Double-page spread in 1938 Museum of Modern Art catalogue with views from west (left) and east (right). *Courtesy of The Museum of Modern Art, New York. Photographs by Luke Swank.*

fig. 9: Views in daytime and at night from
1938 Museum of Modern Art catalogue.
*Courtesy of The Museum of Modern Art,
New York. Photographs by Bill Hedrich.
Chicago History Museum. HB-04414-A3
(top), HB-04414-X2 (bottom).*

in this area, although Kaufmann assumed it would be set on the flatter, east bank of the stream, so as to gain a view of the falls and leave the boulders next to them free for outdoor activities.[7]

Wright, however, had his own idea about where the house should be placed. The decision to site it over the upper waterfall rather than facing it was the critical one in the design process and ultimately determined everything about the perception and meaning of the house. It meant that the house would offer an aural rather than a visual experience of the falling water, an experience that, by its very nature, would be more time-consuming than instantaneous. Wright expressed this intention very clearly. After returning to Wisconsin from Pittsburgh, he wrote to Kaufmann that a design had taken shape in his mind "to the music of the stream."[8]

The temporal dimension of Fallingwater as an expression of virtual, or durational, time was the direct consequence of its having been placed over the waterfall rather than in view of it. In conceiving the design in tune with the movement of the stream for "one who liked to listen to the waterfall," Wright privileged the aural over the visual and thereby gave precedence to the continual over the momentary. Hearing takes time and gives to time a depth that vision lacks. Where looking focuses on that which is present to the eye, listening relies on expectation and is amplified through deferral. Hearing also blurs boundaries and distinctions and renders them fluid in contrast to vision, which specifies, clarifies, and reduces the flux of nature to discrete, controllable, knowable entities. It is thus not by chance, but rather by design, that the visitor to Fallingwater readily confuses the stone with trees, the concrete with water, and the living-room floor with the streambed beneath it.[9]

The dimension of time and its dependence on the sense of hearing play a crucial role in one's experience of the house through both the effects of expectation by deferral and the ambiguity by elision and slippage of sign and signification. The unprecedented use by Wright of large areas of plate glass to mark the boundaries between exterior and interior space creates an openness and transparency that allows for a radical degree of continuity between outside and inside, or nature and architecture (fig. 11). And that interweaving of the two realms was pushed even farther by permitting existing trees to grow through the concrete structure, forcing the beams of the entrance trellis to be curved around some and holes left in the floor of the western terrace to accommodate others (figs. 3 and 8). While some of the trees never survived and others were later replanted, their growth through the building provided, and still provides, a protracted timeline for the architecture. This functions as a measure of the natural cycle of birth, growth, death, and regeneration within which the building is perceived to exist.

If the blurring of boundaries normally separating building and landscape plays a significant role in the perception of Fallingwater, the sense of expectation aroused by deferral is more peculiar to this structure and is impressed upon the visitor from the moment one arrives at the site. The house is approached from the eastern bank of the stream—and, most importantly, from above (fig. 2). As one gets closer to the glen, the structure appears differently at different times of the year. In the early autumn, for instance, it glitters light and dark among the many-colored, turning leaves of the trees. When one nearly reaches the level of the stream, one begins to hear the falls and thus realizes that the house is in direct communication with the water. For the time being, however, it is only heard, not seen.

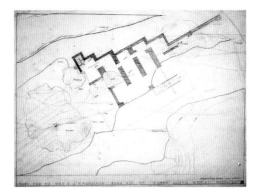

fig. 12　　　　　　　　　　　　　　　　　*fig. 13*

The first full view of the house in its relationship with the water is at the bridge that crosses the stream to the far bank on which the house seems so precariously perched (fig. 7). The bridge is constructed of the same materials of stone and concrete as the house. The walkways to either side of the gravel center are paved with flagstones made from the streambed. It is at this point that one gets one's first view of the water rushing below and the initial sense that there must be a waterfall beyond what can actually be seen. This is known, however, only through the insistent, rushing sound the water makes. At the end of the bridge, the road turns left to pass under the trellis that creates a cavernous space between the wall of the cliff and the rear wall of the house. The house entrance proper is simply a slot in the wall, like a crevice in the cliff. To the left is a tree, growing up through the trellis and the flagstone paving similar to that on the walkways of the bridge.

A sharp left turn after a glass door and up three steps, one finds oneself in the main living space looking across the floor toward the outdoors (fig. 12). The flagstones of the exterior loggia are continued inside, though now waxed and shimmering in the diffused light. The light draws one toward the corner, which opens through floor-to-ceiling glass doors onto a terrace that cantilevers over the falls and provides a deep, raking view of the stream as it descends through the woods to the Youghiogheny River. The diagonal axis bisecting the room follows the direction of the stream below. All Wright's preliminary plans were pivoted in this direction to make the congruence of the visitor's movement and that of the water perspicuous (fig. 13). Only the final drawings, like those in the Museum of Modern Art catalogue, were squared up to the page (fig. 14).

The open plan of the main floor allocates different zones to different functions. It is centered on a square, atrium-like area defined by a recessed ceiling and supporting piers at the corners. At the same time, and more significant for the symbolic expression of the house, is the dynamic definition of the space by the two major diagonal axes that cross at right angles within this square (fig. 14). The first of these diagonals, already noted, is the axis from the entrance to the corner terrace that projects over the falls. The second diagonal extends from the fireplace to the hatch, located just behind the pier marking the corner of the study area. Both diagonals serve to anchor the room to the site, although in different ways.

fig. 12: Living room, diagonal view from entrance to southwest terrace.

fig. 13: Preliminary plan, foundations. *Frank Lloyd Wright Foundation. FLLW FDN # 3603.036*

fig. 14 (right): Plan, ground floor, with overlay of axes from entrance to southwest terrace and fireplace to hatch. *Courtesy of The Museum of Modern Art, New York.*

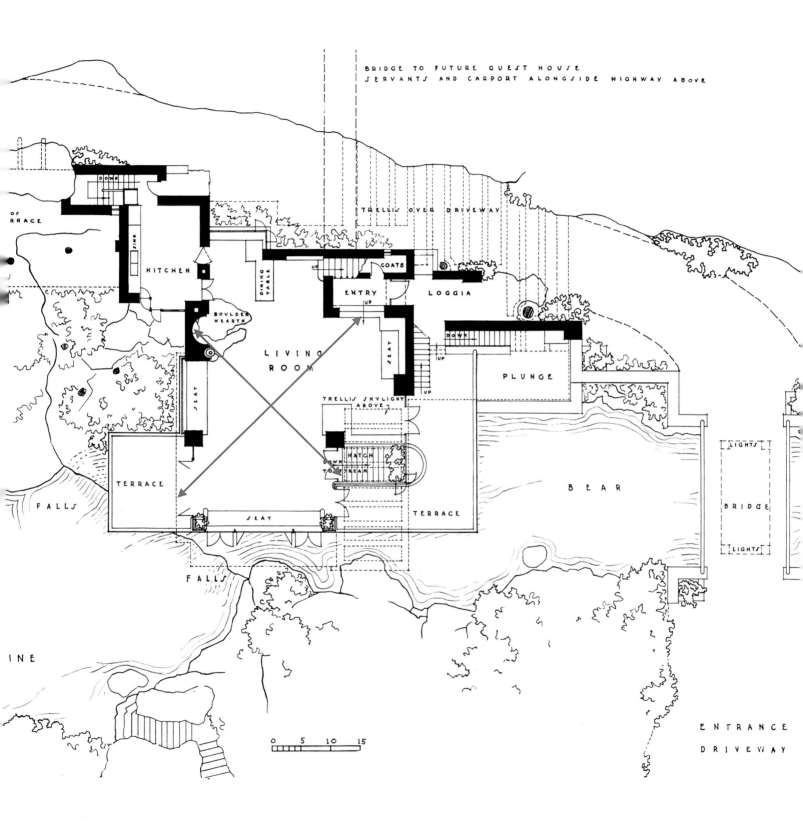

BRIDGE TO FUTURE GUEST HOUSE
SERVANTS AND CARPORT ALONGSIDE HIGHWAY ABOVE

TRELLIS OVER DRIVEWAY

DOWN

OF
RRACE

SINK

KITCHEN

DINING TABLE

UP

COATS

ENTRY

UP

LOGGIA

BOULDER HEARTH

LIVING ROOM

SEAT

UP

SEAT

PLUNGE

DOWN

UP

SEAT

TRELLIS SKYLIGHT ABOVE

DOWN TO STREAM

HATCH

TERRACE

FALLS

SEAT

TERRACE

BEAR

LIGHTS

BRIDGE

LIGHTS

FALLS

INE

ENTRANCE
DRIVEWAY

0   5   10   15

fig. 15: Livingroom fireplace.

fig. 16

The fireplace is the most prominent vertical element in the room (fig. 15). It is built upon the living rock of the boulder that forms part of the house's foundations (fig. 16). The boulder itself protrudes through the flagstone flooring to become the hearth. It was left unwaxed to establish its continuity with the living rock and thus differentiate it from the cut and polished stone flooring. A cavity in the left pier of the fireplace contains a spherical cast-iron kettle that was designed to swing out over the fire to allow the Kaufmanns to mull wine, cider, or other such things. Whether that was part of the program is not known. What is known, however, is that Wright wanted such a device, even if only for water, in order to produce both an audible and palpable sense of liquid in the room. "The warming kettle," he reportedly told his apprentices, "will swing into the fire, boiling the water. Steam will permeate the atmosphere. You'll hear the hiss."[10]

The hatch terminates the second diagonal axis of the space just behind the study, between it and the terrace facing the bridge (figs. 17 and 18). Its formal link to the fireplace is made explicit by the fact that these two features are the only ones in the house incorporating a semicircular form.[11] In the fireplace, the interior cavity forms a half-cylinder; in the hatch, there is a corresponding half-cylindrical parapet, cut into the terrace. It functions, as we will see, as an echo chamber. The hatch is also similar to the fireplace in that it serves to bring the outdoors into the room. Above it is a skylight-trellis. Even more significantly, at floor level it opens to the rushing water below. The steel and glass enclosure is composed of three horizontal panes that telescope back while a pair of glass doors in the front swing apart to bring into view a flight of steps suspended from steel rods and leading down to the water.

While it may have originally been justified as a way for the Kaufmanns to go for a dip in the stream directly from the living room, the hatch had a more profound importance for Wright. When his client protested against the expenditure for an item that might never really be used, the architect shot back: "We got down into the glen to associate directly with the stream and planned the house for that association. Hence the steps from living room to stream." "This feature," Wright asserted, was absolutely "necessary from every standpoint."[12] The open hatch, it should be noted, provides the only view of the water from inside the space of the living room. It is merely a passing glimpse, however, that adds to the increasing sense of expectation.

fig. 16: Boulder beneath fireplace under living-room floor.

fig. 17 (right): Hatch.

fig. 18: Steps leading down to stream from hatch with concrete supports of living room on left.

fig. 20

The stairs descending from the hatch end in a platform that hovers just above the waterline to establish the lowest plane in the series of horizontal terraces and layers that overlap one another and interlock with one another as the house rises above the stream through the trees. Contrary to what one might have expected, the generous outdoor living spaces at Fallingwater do not afford more and better views of the landscape the higher they rise. Rather, they provide an ever-increasing sense of being engulfed by the forest and becoming part of the natural environment it creates (fig. 6). It is a multisensory experience in which the purely optical or visual is, once again, downplayed in favor of what one might best describe as a kind of natural effect of the forest's "surround sound."

The full expression of Fallingwater and the experience of spatial movement through it were only completely realized when the garage and guest house were built farther up the hillside in 1938–39 (fig. 19). Wright extended the drive under the trellis and beyond the westernmost terrace of the house before curving it back on itself to climb to the next level, where it ends in a four-car garage that forms the north-south wing of the L-shaped structure. The guest house itself is set at right angles to the garage to parallel the main house below. It stretches out along the upper ridge and terminates in a tank-like pool that is filled nearly to the brim, appearing heavy with water and about to overflow. That sense of water brimming over and being channeled down the hillside is given physical expression in the folded plate roof of the canopied walk that connects the guest house to the main house and provides cover for those descending from the one to the other.

The image of water rippling down the slope echoes, in architectural terms, the actual water coursing under the house itself and thus leads us to understand Fallingwater as an active participant in the landscape, metaphorically representing the descent of Bear Run at the same time as it incorporates the stream into its own space and structure. In its embodiment of the movement of water in both symbolic and real terms, Fallingwater thus gives substance to its name and makes one aware that the passage of time involved in that movement is the critical element in the reception of the building. This returns us to the issue of the expression of virtual, or durational, time in Fallingwater suggested as early as 1938 in the Museum of Modern Art's pairing of the same view of the house in daytime and at night.

fig. 19 (left): Aerial view of house (at right side) and guest house (at left side) with connecting canopy.

fig. 20: Guest house pool.

Fallingwater as an Image of Time

We saw how the approach to the house and the movement around and through it constantly postpone the view of the falls in order to allow the sound of the water, and the understanding of the environment they create, to sink into our consciousness. We also saw how the architecture elides with the environment so as to make the distinction between nature and building a matter of degree rather than kind and thus embed the man-made forms of the building in the larger time-frame of natural growth. And, finally, we saw how the blurring of the boundary between nature and architecture is mirrored by the blurring of the distinction between outside and inside, as the flagstone paving of the bridge and entrance area carries over into the floor of the main interior space of the house.

It is in this space, as one might expect, and in large part due to the treatment of the floor, that the sense of movement of the water underneath, and the virtual time that movement suggests, first become apparent to the visitor (fig. 12). Like the flagstones on the exterior, the ones inside are made from stones taken from the streambed. But unlike those outdoors, the ones in the living room are waxed and polished so as to reflect the light and give the appearance of a slippery, fast-moving surface replicating that of the streambed directly beneath it (figs. 17 and 21). Everything about the treatment of this paving, from the irregularity of its surface to the swirling, raised lines of the grout, works to convey a sense of congruence with its natural referent.[13]

The initial visual impression builds to a more complex and multisensory one as one walks across the surface toward the light. One feels kinesthetically a sense of moving water underfoot, and that fluid motion is transmitted to the body, as it were, from the ground up. The fireplace on the right and the hatch on the left reinforce the connection to the stream and waterfalls at the same time as they mark the passage of time in one's movement across the room. The projection of the living rock through the floor at the hearth, in contrast to the descent of the stairs to the stream through the floor of the hatch, brings to mind the drop of the falls from one level to the next and situates the visitor or occupant in the space and time in between.

The hatch is the most important element in imparting to the room this sense of virtual time. It is also the most unusual and most surprising. When open, it provides not only a glimpse of the water but also, and much more powerfully, the sound, smell, and physical sense of moisture. It underscores the waxed flagstones of the floor and allows the element of moving water to pervade the space of the room. But ultimately, it is the aural aspect that is the most important. Hearing the water constantly rushing underneath—amplified by the effect of the echo chamber-like semicircular backing of the hatch—extends the kinesthetic experience of the constructed interior space into a temporal dimension that includes the entire physical environment of which that space is a part.[14] Through hearing, one imagines what one might see, and it is this that gives Fallingwater a valence beyond the momentary and the purely visual. Inside the space of the room, one already senses the continuous and unending cycle of nature—of growth, movement, and change—that the view of the house from below the falls ultimately confirms, although only after one has left the house, descended the path along the south bank, and stopped to look back (fig. 3).

fig. 21

fig. 21: Streambed below first falls.

fig. 22 (right): Bear Run upstream from house.

fig. 24

fig. 25

fig. 26

As an integral part of its natural environment, Fallingwater appears as mutable as the landscape. It registers its effects and continually changes with the seasons. In the fall, the autumn leaves bring out a burnished quality in the pale apricot color of the painted concrete, while the falls slowly diminish to a mere trickle as winter comes along (fig. 23). In winter, when the ice takes over, the house itself seems to become frozen in time (fig. 24), only to return to life, with a vengeance, with the early spring rains. Such an engagement on the part of architecture with the elements of nature is extraordinary and sets Fallingwater apart. To animate, activate, and give life to buildings, architects have often used water in the form of fountains (fig. 25). But while the water may be natural, the shape and movement imparted to it are artificial and man-made. The liveliness is merely an illusion. More to the point, the illusion, like that of a play, only lasts for a limited amount of time. Eventually, the fountain is turned off and all becomes static once again (fig. 26). As in the theater, when the play ends and the lights come back on, the audience is made aware of the gulf between art and reality—which is to say, art and life.

The extraordinary thing about Fallingwater is that the illusion, the spectacle, the movement of water never stops. This may sound simplistic, but it is profound. Once it gets dark, and especially after the lights in the house have been turned off, one naturally expects the falls to be turned off as well—but they cannot be (fig. 27). Fallingwater is continuous with the stream and waterfalls that preceded it and with the entire natural system that has grown up around them and takes its life from them. The experience of the house is an experience of time as duration. Wright used to like to say that in his own house, Taliesin, you could not easily "tell where pavements and walls left off and ground began."[15] In Fallingwater, by contrast, you do not ask where the house ends and the natural environment begins. Instead, you ask when—and the answer is never. This finally is what gives the building its magic, its uniqueness, and its lasting significance. The house is, as the architect Paul Rudolph once wrote, a "realized dream."[16] It is a palpable mental space where time both expands and contracts independent of one's volition and not always fully comprehensible to the conscious mind, though always and inevitably in tune with natural laws.

fig. 23 (left): View from below second falls in early autumn.

fig. 24: View from below second falls in winter.

fig. 25: Fountain of Latona, garden of Château of Versailles, seventeenth century. Photo by author.

fig. 26: Fountain of Latona. Photo by author.

fig. 27: View from bridge at night.

FALLINGWATER'S INTERIORS: RUSTIC ELEGANCE AND FLEXIBLE LIVING

By Justin Gunther

In creating Fallingwater, Wright and the Kaufmanns collaborated to construct a place of repose where the family could escape the city for renewal in nature. Ever present is an interaction between interior and exterior that promotes a powerful interplay between the comforts of home and the natural world. The Kaufmanns appreciated the intense connection to nature the architecture afforded, and they adapted to Wright's design, creating a country house with rusticity and sophistication.

With the systems of Wright's architecture—stone, glass, steel, and woodwork—defining the backdrop, the Kaufmanns decorated Fallingwater with eclectic tastes and a discerning eye. The objects that fill Fallingwater represent a lifetime of collecting, and notions of flexibility and informality governed the Kaufmanns' assemblage and arrangement of art. Their relaxed, yet refined, approach harmonized with Wright's modernism and provided the essential personal touch to complete the composition. Tracing the evolution of the collection—from Wright, through the Kaufmanns, to the Western Pennsylvania Conservancy—reveals the themes that created one of the world's most dynamic interiors.

Wright's Backdrop

Wright defined the background for decoration, choosing materiality and coloration with great restraint and precision. He carried the stone and concrete of the exterior inside to create a neutral palette of gray and rosy ocher. The only other color was his signature Cherokee red, specified for all metal surfaces. Liliane Kaufmann initially found this limited color scheme "cold, barren, and monotonous," but she quickly became accustomed to its beautiful simplicity, writing that the painted concrete served as "a quiet background" for artwork. The calm tones of the stone and concrete paralleled the broad swaths of color in nature, and like wildflowers and songbirds set against masses of green and brown in the woods, the Kaufmanns' art and vivid textiles were meant to animate spaces with accents of color.[1]

Complementing the subtlety of the interior backdrop was Wright's choice of architectural ornament. Curved metal shelves, a spherical fireplace kettle, shield-shaped trellis lights, and dentils in light screens were understated and rigorously integrated with the building. True ornament, Wright believed, should exist as "the inherent melody of structure," as the "manifest abstract pattern of structure itself."[2] Fallingwater's ornament does just that by responding throughout to the plasticity of the reinforced concrete, the horizontality of the cantilevers, and the nuances of the landscape.

Most important, nature rather than manufactured ornament is maintained as the interior's primary enlivener. Broad bands of windows open the house to countless perspectives, and as Edgar Kaufmann jr. wrote, "Attention is directed toward the outside by low ceilings; no lordly hall sets the tone but, instead, the luminous textures of the woodlands, rhythmically enframed." The windows' steel framework articulates nature, producing a patterned view of the landscape that Kaufmann jr. and others likened to folding Japanese screens changed out with the seasons.[3]

Wright designed over 160 pieces of freestanding and built-in furniture to complete the composition of his interior. Manufactured by the Gillen Woodworking Corporation of Milwaukee, the furniture was constructed of marine-quality plywood to resist warping, and veneered with North

fig. 1

fig. 2

page 216: Jacques Lipchitz's *Harpist* in the third-floor gallery.

fig. 1: Edgar Kaufmann jr. relaxing in nature on the living room's east terrace. *Western Pennsylvania Conservancy.*

fig. 2: Edgar Kaufmann Sr. with dachshund enjoying the living room soon after the house's completion in 1938. *Western Pennsylvania Conservancy.*

fig. 3 (right): View of Edgar Kaufmann Sr.'s bedroom. Floor-to-ceiling windows minimize the boundary between interior and exterior space. Views of the landscape are architecturally framed by the folding steel sash. Featured in this space is the Butterfly Chair by designers Bonet, Kurchan, and Ferrari-Hardoy.

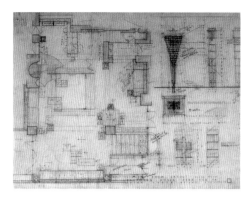

fig. 5

Carolina black walnut. Wright regarded wood "as the most humanely intimate of all materials," and the rich brown of the walnut offered a warm contrast to the sandstone and concrete surfaces. To add interest and visually reinforce the lines of the house, Wright retained sapwood in his veneers, carefully book-matching the streaks to create stunning highlights.[4]

Furthering the continuity between architecture and interior decoration, Wright integrated primary design motifs into the furniture to echo the building's structural themes. The horizontal line predominates and gives the furniture a rhythm and humanized scale that promotes interaction and relaxation. Paying homage to the cantilevers, table tops flair out from supports of interacting planes, and long sofas built against walls seem to float. The cascading shelves of the partners desk evoke the overlapping structural trays of the house. And quarter-circle openings in desktops, rounded shelves, and bullnosed edges all balance with the house's rounded rooflines and parapet walls.

By using seating of varying heights and proportioning it lower to the ground, Wright planned an environment conducive to people's natural patterns of gathering and conversation. In addition to the fixed sofas, Wright designed two types of movable seats—higher hassocks with a cabinetry frame and lower zabutons, named after a type of Japanese floor pillow. At Edgar Kaufmann jr.'s suggestion, cushions were made of Dunlopillo, vulcanized liquid latex honeycombed with air bubbles. The latex foam provided durability and ventilation and represented the first residential application of the material.[5]

Backs and seats of sofas were originally upholstered in a beige monk's cloth, and the Kaufmanns tried red, green, yellow, and blue on the moveable furniture before settling on red and yellow. When not in use, zabutons and hassocks were arranged consonant with the architecture, in asymmetrical patterns suggesting movement. The vivid red and yellow brought color into the realm of spatial accentuation, and the "free-floating seats," Kaufmann jr. said, served as "signposts of space . . . [allowing] the eye to measure distances and areas by providing reference points." The splashes of color also helped to loosen up the interior, reducing emphasis on finite points and directing attention to a myriad of views.[6]

The Kaufmanns embraced the majority of Wright's vision for the interior; however, they

fig. 4 (left): Sapwood lines in the wall-hung wardrobes of the master bedroom emphasize the architecture's horizontality. *fig. 5:* Living room furnishing plan, circa 1936, proposed by Wright. Drawn in blue pencil is the proposed light standard which the Kaufmanns rejected. *The Frank Lloyd Wright Foundation. FLLW FDN # 3602.078*

fig. 6: Partners desk in the living room. The four design motifs found throughout the house (horizontal lines, cantilevers, circles and semi-circles, and cascading elements) are found in the desk and unify the elements within the space. Located next to the stairs to the stream, the desk's bottom lozenge-shaped shelf also neatly echoes the shape of the hatch's concrete opening.

fig. 7: A furniture grouping beside the living room fireplace. Zabutons (left) and hassocks (right) were loosely arranged to facilitate comfort and conversation.

fig. 8: The master bedroom fireplace displays some of the house's most dramatic stonework, including a niche for the family's fifteenth-century Madonna and Child. To the right on the rock shelf are two samples of experimental music printing by Paul Koch. The picture frame and lamp on the desk are Tiffany, and the peasant chair is English. In the corner by the door is an upholstered slipper chair by László Gábor and a Hiroshige woodblock of an iris garden, a Christmas gift from Wright.

fig. 9: The diversity of the Kaufmanns' collection is apparent throughout. In this corner of the living room, visitors encounter Florentine peasant chairs around a Wright-designed dining table; a portrait of Edgar Kaufmann Sr. by Austrian-born Victor Hammer hanging above a Burmese wedding chest; and shelves displaying a varied range of objects, including a German woodstove model (top shelf), an Indian incense burner (top shelf), a Zuni Pueblo pot (third shelf), a Danish vase by Axel Salto (second shelf), and a Pennsylvania earthenware flower pot (bottom shelf).

did reject rugs, barrel chairs, and light standards planned for the living room. Wright designed area rugs to accentuate spaces and mirror features, like the central ceiling light fixture. While the Kaufmanns used their long-haired dachshunds as an excuse, the underlying reason for rejection was a desire for informality. Instead of site-specific rugs, they decided on a looser scattering of tribal Moroccan rugs and large animal fur throws made from locally trapped skunks and raccoons. The barrel chairs proposed for the dining table further competed with easy-going country life. The Kaufmanns disliked the chairs' strictness and rigidity, substituting rustic three-legged peasant chairs found in Florence. To light the living room at night, Wright suggested distributing lamp standards around the room. Wright created two different designs; the Kaufmanns rejected both, arguing they introduced an odd solemnity and nervousness to an otherwise peaceful space.[7]

The Kaufmanns did accept a scattering of smaller task lamps, on desks and beside beds, to provide supplemental light for reading and writing. Wright attached pivoting shades of black walnut—long and horizontal for desks and short and vertical for bedsides—to bases of patinated bronze. The remainder of lighting was indirect and integrated with the architecture, concealed behind wooden shields atop cabinetry or behind muslin-covered ceiling screens. At the recommendation of Edgar Kaufmann jr., Wright used fluorescent tubes, a new product in the 1930s. Fluorescents provided an even, continuous light and, when reflected off the warm-tinted ocher of the ceiling, produced a soft, calming effect.[8]

Kaufmanns' Collection

By the end of 1937, Fallingwater was largely completed, and the Kaufmanns began enjoying their weekend retreat. Some woodwork and final touches were not finished until 1938, and the guest house and servants' quarters would come later in 1939. Nevertheless, Wright had set the primary scheme for the interior, and the family began decorating by following the architect's lead. In his memoir of Fallingwater, Edgar Kaufmann jr. credits his mother as the primary decorator, stating that Liliane's "wide-ranging tastes and keen attention to detail allowed her to improvise with grace and individuality."[9] However, more than Liliane's hand was at play. The collection amassed for Fallingwater was a collaborative family effort and included objects acquired through retailing, travel, associations, and friendships.

While the majority of objects were new purchases, a number were imported from their earlier houses. Large-scale Audubons from the 1831 double-elephant folio and chestnut-stump side tables, which Wright disliked because of their upside-down orientation, were brought from the Hangover, the Kaufmanns' original cabin at Bear Run. As reminders of La Torelle, their Benno Janssen–designed manor in the Pittsburgh suburbs, they displayed a wrought-iron fireplace fork and an elaborate candlestick, both crafted by Samuel Yellin, and a sculpture of the Madonna and Child. The centuries-old wooden sculpture came to the family through the New York firm of French & Company, renowned dealers of European art, and was a favorite of Liliane's. The work was given special prominence in Fallingwater, displayed in a niche Wright designed within the stonework of the master bedroom fireplace.[10]

In buying for Fallingwater, the Kaufmanns collected with well-cultivated and confident

fig. 10: Richmond Barthé's statue of Rose McClendon on the stone wall of the stepped canopy.

fig. 12

fig. 13

fig. 11 (left): The *Virgen de Guadalupe*, now hanging at Fallingwater, was previously shown at the Vendôme shops of Kaufmann's department store during the *Below the Rio Grande* exhibition.

fig. 12: László Gábor (left) and family friend, A. James Speyer (right), on the living room's west terrace, circa 1938. *Western Pennsylvania Conservancy.*

fig. 13: *Below the Rio Grande* exhibition in the Vendôme shops of Kaufmann's department store. On the wall is the painting of the *Virgen de Guadalupe* (transferred to Fallingwater after the exhibit and shown in photograph at left). Just below it is a majolica vase, currently displayed in the guest house. *Western Pennsylvania Conservancy.*

tastes, and ownership of Pittsburgh's largest department store presented the family with an almost limitless outlet. As innovative retailers with close ties to New York and Europe, the Kaufmanns embraced the latest trends. Their commitment to art was evidenced by their 1930 remodel of the department store's main floor, which incorporated dramatic, chic interiors designed by Benno Janssen and a series of murals entitled the *History of Commerce* by Boardman Robinson. At the unveiling, Edgar Kaufmann's speech revealed his opinion that "the development of art should be the cultural goal of America . . . . As a general appreciation of beauty grows, we are prompted and inspired to cherish more and more zealously the principles of art and the laws of harmony."[11]

Liliane championed this cause by taking over the store's unprofitable eleventh floor. In 1933 she opened the Vendôme shops, named after the elegant Place Vendôme in Paris, to offer sophisticated customers a high-quality selection of tasteful goods. Rather than stylistic homogeneity, Liliane stressed a causal attitude toward style, offering a creative mix of high style and craft, from modern to antique.[12]

This was an aesthetic the family carried over to Fallingwater and explains the rich diversity of their collection. The Kaufmanns felt variety, flexibility, and comfort complemented not only a country lifestyle but also Wright's naturalized modernism, which expressed freedom in design and an organic approach to form and materials. Furthermore, the refinement of the architecture created an extremely accepting interior, one that embraced the Kaufmanns' relaxed and elegant sensibilities. With diverse tastes, they bought objects dating to a wide range of eras and an even broader range of national and ethnic origins—over thirty different countries and cultures are represented in the living room alone.[13] Many of these items were acquired during buying trips, coordinated with the store's offices in New York, London, Paris, Florence, and Vienna. Some shopping was done much closer to home, in the mountains of Appalachia, where they bought local craft pieces, such as milk glass, Pennsylvania painted farm chairs, and salt-glazed stoneware.[14]

Edgar and Liliane's retailing connections in New York and abroad cultivated their son's interest in art, and from 1927 to 1935, Kaufmann jr. pursued a broad and unconventional education. During that period he studied painting in New York, attended the Kunstgewerbeschule in Vienna,

<figure>*fig. 14*</figure>

apprenticed under Viennese artist Victor Hammer in Florence and London, and joined Wright's fellowship at Taliesin. Lasting friendships were made during this coming of age, many of which impacted Fallingwater.

His time in New York was facilitated by his childhood mentor, W. Frank Purdy, who headed the Ferargil Galleries.[15] Purdy helped introduce Kaufmann jr. to the New York scene, and among the artists he befriended was the Harlem Renaissance sculptor Richmond Barthé. Four portrait sculptures by Barthé made their way to Fallingwater: a statue of the renowned, African-American stage actress Rose McClendon and busts of Kaufmann jr., an unknown boy, and W. Frank Purdy. The spirituality and repose of Barthé's McClendon blended perfectly with the house's landscape, and Kaufmann jr. felt it "should stand nearly hidden in some haphazard spot, to be discovered now and then, or sought out—but not displayed." Its placement, partially hidden amidst the rhododendron of the stepped canopy, complemented the work's drama and serenity.[16]

While in Vienna, he cultivated a friendship with Hungarian-born painter László Gábor. In 1935 the family helped Gábor immigrate to the United States and employed him as the store's art director. In addition to designing product displays and shop windows, Gábor created comfortable furniture for Fallingwater, of which only one chair—a slipper chair in the master bedroom—survives.[17] Gábor later assisted others in Austria with the immigration process. Of particular note was Josef Frank, who organized an exhibition at Kaufmann's in 1951 of his furnishings designed for the Swedish firm Svenskt Tenn. The leather-seated chair by Frank in Edgar Sr.'s bedroom was purchased through this association.[18]

A great appreciation for Victor Hammer's talent motivated Kaufmann jr. to apprentice with the artist from 1930 to 1933. Liliane made the introduction, having met Hammer in London in 1929, where she commissioned the portrait of her husband entitled *Excursion* now hanging in Fallingwater's living room. Hammer had set up an artists' workshop in Florence, the Stamperia del Santuccio, and along with painting, Kaufmann jr. studied bookbinding, printing, and calligraphy. Punchcutter Paul Koch was also in residence, and Kaufmann jr. worked with him on a reprint of Milton's *Samson Agonistes*. The senior Kaufmanns adored Koch and were flattered

fig. 14: Souvenir postcard image of Liliane Kaufmann shopping in a Mexican bazaar, 1940s. *Western Pennsylvania Conservancy.*

fig. 15 (right): Mexican pottery and Pre-Columbian figures on the cantilevered shelves of the guest house.

by his gifts of experimental music printing, which they treasured and displayed in Fallingwater's master bedroom.[19]

After Hammer, Kaufmann jr. enrolled in Wright's apprenticeship program at Taliesin, entranced by the architect's philosophy after reading his recently published autobiography. Although he only spent a brief six months at Taliesin, his experience there cemented the family's tie to Wright and set the Fallingwater commission in motion. By April of 1935, Kaufmann jr. had returned to Pittsburgh to take his long-deferred place in the family store. As merchandise manager for the home department, he played a pivotal role in integrating the family's interest in art with business, particularly through exhibitions. In 1938 Kaufmann jr. began an association with the Museum of Modern Art, enlisting the department store as a site for the museum's newly instituted program of traveling exhibitions. The store also organized shows internally, and in 1940 Kaufmann jr. and Liliane presented *Below the Rio Grande*, an exhibition of Mexican antiques and folk art. Items displayed were offered for sale and several unsold pieces went to Fallingwater, including the painting *Virgen de Guadalupe* at the top of the stairs, milk glass bottles decorated with the Mexican coat of arms in Liliane's bathroom, and majolica vases in the guest house.[20]

This interest in Latin American culture emerged from numerous trips, and Liliane frequently expressed her fondness for Mexico, once stating, "I have never seen so much sheer natural beauty added to so much that is old and interesting."[21] The family's wealth and connections provided entrance to the country's elite artist circles. Diego Rivera and Frida Kahlo became family friends, which explains Rivera's Conté crayon *Profile of a Man Wearing a Hat* in the guest bedroom and his *Torrid Siesta (El Sueño)* watercolor in the bridge. Rivera introduced the Kaufmanns to sculptor Mardonio Magaña, and the family was taken by his rough-hewn folk compositions. They purchased four of his works, one in wood and three in stone, to complement Fallingwater's rusticity. Another acquisition tied to Rivera was the purchase of an 1877 painting entitled *Landscape: Jalapa, Mexico* by José María Velasco. The artist had been Rivera's mentor and was regarded as Mexico's greatest landscape painter. Outside of fine art, the Kaufmanns bought Mayan pre-Columbian figures, small religious paintings on tin called *recuerdas*, and countless pieces of pottery in bazaars and antique shops throughout Mexico.[22]

By further cultivating his connections at MoMA, through his work on Eliot Noyes' 1941 exhibition *Organic Design in Home Furnishings* and as a member of the architecture and industrial design committees during his war service, Kaufmann jr. eventually became head of the museum's industrial design department and later the director of the Good Design program of 1950–55. Under the auspices of "good design" and the tastemaking authority of MoMA, Kaufmann jr. headed juries to select items for exhibition at Chicago's Merchandise Mart and MoMA. Products meeting the requirements of good design "merged form and function" and demonstrated "an awareness of human values expressed in relation to industrial production for a democratic society." Among those featured in the exhibitions were Louis Comfort Tiffany, Alvar Aalto, Gunnel Nyman, Kaj Franck, Saara Hopea, Timo Sarpaneva, Jorge Ferrari-Hardoy, Bruno Mathsson and Finn Juhl. [23]

Kaufmann jr. brought "good design" home to Fallingwater, integrating works by these artists and designers into Fallingwater's furnishings. Just about every room is decorated with one or more

pieces by Tiffany in bronze and Favrile glass, the most remarkable being the Mandarin table lamp Kaufmann jr. placed in his mother's bedroom. He appreciated both the lamp's beauty and structure, comparing the strengthened form of the shade's folded veining to the house's folded concrete slabs.[24] Beautifully blown pieces of Scandinavian glass, appearing with almost as much frequency as Tiffany objects, included iconic Savoy vases by Aalto, richly colored bowls in amethyst and sapphire by Franck, nesting tumblers by Hopea, an amorphous crystal ashtray by Nyman, a tri-color vase by Sarpaneva, and a unique glass sphere with internal filaments also by Sarpaneva.

Pertaining to chairs, one of the most talked about is the Butterfly Chair on display in Edgar Sr.'s bedroom designed in Buenos Aires by Bonet, Kurchan and Ferrari-Hardoy. Kaufmann jr. called this Butterfly Chair the "granddaddy of them all," since it was one of the first brought into the United States. Kaufmann jr. purchased others for the MoMA collection, and after exhibiting the Butterfly Chair there it became immensely poplar and spawned countless derivatives.[25]

Bruno Mathsson and Finn Juhl, whose respective bentwood lounge and 45 Chair are in Fallingwater, also owe much to Kaufmann jr. for their popularity. Through MoMA and the Good Design shows, Kaufmann jr. helped introduce these Scandinavian designers to the American market. He admired their furniture for its duality of craft and industry and praised their designs for "revealing a practical, uncomplicated sensible beauty." As shown by the ease with which they relate to Fallingwater, their chairs represented an honest approach to materials, simplicity of line, integration of decoration and structure, and balance of proportions. For Kaufmann jr., these chairs also served as comforting reminders of the strong friendships he cultivated with Mathsson and Juhl.[26]

Another friendship with ties to the Good Design exhibitions was Kaufmann jr.'s close relationship with A. James Speyer. At Kaufmann jr.'s request, the installation of the Good Design exhibitions at the Merchandise Mart in 1954 and 1955, and at MoMA in 1955, were directed by Speyer, a talented young architect with an eye for exhibition design. Like Kaufmann jr., Speyer had grown up in Pittsburgh, and his parents, Tillie and Alexander, were some of Edgar Sr. and Liliane's closest friends. The families frequently enjoyed weekends together at Fallingwater and shared a passion for art and collecting. Their aesthetics often overlapped, and the Kaufmanns displayed gifts

fig. 16: Window display from one of Edgar Kaufmann jr.'s *Good Design* exhibitions. *Western Pennsylvania Conservancy.*

fig. 17   fig. 18

from the Speyers throughout the house, including a large glass lens over the entry door, a French rooster weathervane, and Mexican copper trays. [27]

In addition to James, other Speyers were accomplished in the arts. Tillie Speyer took up sculpture later in life, primarily in stone, and a stylized, spiral marble work by her rests on the desk in the guest house bedroom. Nora, James's sister, became an accomplished painter, and while her work does not hang in Fallingwater, a painting by her husband, Sideo Fromboluti, can be found in the guest house. Entitled *August*, Fromboluti's abstracted landscape in heavy impasto complements the house's textures and provides contrast to Velasco's more academic landscape hanging just opposite. [28]

The Kaufmanns' relationship with Wright influenced the collection as well. On occasional visits throughout the 1950s, Wright frequently made recommendations, particularly for modern sculpture placement. As Kaufmann jr. recalled, he would ask "to have statues relocated, often only a few feet from where they were . . . into a telling position, where it accentuated a feature of the architecture." The orientation of Jacques Lipchitz's *Mother and Child* on the wall of the plunge pool was once turned 180 degrees at Wright's request. Although outspoken about the sculpture, Wright, as Kaufmann jr. remembered, "never made a sarcastic remark about these works, nor attempted to persuade us to other tastes." The architect held intense respect for the family's understanding of his architecture and clearly accepted their approach to decorating with modern sculpture. In addition to *Mother and Child*, the collection grew to include Marino Marini's *The Horseman*, Jacques Lipchitz's *The Harpist*, Peter Voulkos's *Funiculated Smog*, Auguste Rodin's *Iris*, and Joseph Goto's *Landscape in the Air*. [29]

Through the gift of six Japanese woodblock prints by Hokusai and Hiroshige, Wright extended his love of Asian art to Fallingwater. The Kaufmanns do not credit Wright, but their collection of Asian sculpture—including guardian lion tomb panels, a cast-iron Buddha head, and ceramics, such as Ming Dynasty teapots and Imari plates—was likely influenced by visits to Taliesin. There they would have admired Wright's extensive Asian collection and also the arrangements of greenery and flowers that harmonized with the artwork and architecture. At Fallingwater, this

fig. 17: Liliane Kaufmann (left) with Tillie Speyer (right) at the guest house swimming pool, 1938. *Western Pennsylvania Conservancy.*

fig. 18: A. James Speyer smoking poolside, Darthea Speyer sunbathing on the trellis, and Tillie Speyer reclined and reading at the guest house, all enjoying the relaxed spirit of Fallingwater, early 1940s. *Western Pennsylvania Conservancy.*

fig. 19 (right): Desk in the guest house bedroom. Hanging above is Sideo Fromboluti's *August* and on the desk is a marble sculpture by Tillie Speyer. The barrel chair is Wright's prototype for the dining table in the main house, which the Kaufmanns decided not to use.

fig. 20: Ming Dynasty teapots and Imari plates displayed on the built-in sideboard and Canton ware rice bowls on the streamlined metal shelves are evidence of the Kaufmanns' interest in Asian antiques.

fig. 21

tradition manifested itself through displays of fresh-cut flowers, always of one color and variety, taking inspiration from both Wright's practices and Liliane's love of cutting gardens.[30]

The Kaufmanns also visited Wright at Taliesin West in Arizona. These travels, in addition to vacationing in Palm Springs, cultivated an interest in Native American basketry and pottery of the Southwest. In various locations throughout the house, they accessorized with Zuni and San Ildefonso Pueblo pots and Pomo tribal baskets.[31]

Stewardship

Edgar Sr. and Liliane passed away in the 1950s and Kaufmann jr. held on to Fallingwater until 1963, at which point he donated the house and land to the Western Pennsylvania Conservancy. Fallingwater opened as a house museum, with the conservancy acting as the primary steward; however, Kaufmann jr. maintained ownership of the collection and edited Fallingwater's interiors with curatorial sensibilities. He exercised greater scrutiny than his parents but preserved their spirit of diversity.

Along with concerns about presentation were personal attachments to particular works and worries about the new museum's resources to conserve fine art. Noteworthy objects that left Fallingwater, some going to his house in Garrison, New York, others to his apartment in Manhattan, included Joan Miró's *The Cat*, Piet Mondrian's *Diagonal*, Theodoros Stamos's *Greek Orison*, a sketch of a man by Amedeo Modigliani, a painting by Frida Kahlo, an etching by Paul Klee, drawings by Peter Blume, and Auguste Rodin's *Iris*.[32] As Kaufmann jr. watched the museum mature, he gifted works to enhance the house's appearance. A sampling of the fine art he added include two Picasso aquatints, Lyonel Feininger's *Church on the Cliffs VII*, a brass relief by Luisa Rota, and Bryan Hunt's *Bear Run I*. Hunt's piece was commissioned in the late 1970s to fill the long-standing void created by the loss of Marino Marini's *The Horseman* during a 1956 flash flood.[33]

Regarding textiles, Kaufmann jr. thought the "rugs, bedspreads, upholstery, and other textiles that add color everywhere" should be "restored and replaced" to maintain the freshness and residential character of the house. He actively acquired Moroccan rugs for the floors, tribal ikats

fig. 21: View of the living room, likely taken in the early 1960s. The Miró to the right of the dining table is one of the works Edgar Kaufmann jr. removed from Fallingwater. *Western Pennsylvania Conservancy.*

fig. 22

fig. 23

for draping, and spirited patterns for pillows, and curators have carried on this collecting tradition. The Kaufmanns frequently reupholstered, and under Kaufmann jr.'s guidance the furniture was last redone in the 1980s with Jack Lenor Larsen's Doria fabric.[34]

For the conservancy's management of Fallingwater, Kaufmann jr. stressed flexibility, stating the house's "character does not depend on particular objects in fixed places, but on a sensitive, flexible response to what was the original atmosphere of Fallingwater." The objects were "merely accoutrements of pleasant living," "this's and that's" collected "out of friendship and liking for the things themselves, and brought in to simply make things more personal." In interpreting the house, the collection should be subordinate "to the real values present."[35]

The conservancy strives to honor this philosophy through its interpretation of the house, focusing on the message of Wright's architecture and using the collection to reveal side stories about the family. Above all, the collection shows that "a Wright house uses and favors fine art," and by decorating in the same spirit that formed the architecture, the Kaufmanns contributed to a unified composition of building and nature.

fig. 22: Auguste Rodin's *Iris* was once displayed on the stone retaining wall at the guest house swimming pool. *Western Pennsylvania Conservancy.*

fig. 23: Jacques Lipchitz's *Mother and Child* on the wall of the plunge pool. The orientation shown was suggested by Wright, which the Kaufmanns later changed by turning the sculpture 180 degrees. *Western Pennsylvania Conservancy.*

fig. 24 (right): Jacques Lipchitz's *Mother and Child* on the wall of the plunge pool.

FALLINGWATER: INTEGRATED ARCHITECTURE'S MODERN LEGACY AND SUSTAINABLE PROSPECT

By John M. Reynolds

In a way, the Europeans and those American architects who embraced the modernist aesthetic were right about Wright's not being a "modern man" within their terms, so strong in him was the insistence on the experience of nature and of site as the wellspring of creative form-giving. It is possible to show however . . . that the same values generated by a widely shared mythic conception of the American nation and of nature—that shaped both Olmsted's and Wright's sensibilities as children of the nineteenth century, endure in our own day and still find expression in literature, the visual arts, cinema, music—and architecture.

—Catherine Howett

Seventy-five years after its inception, Fallingwater affirms architecture's prospect to engage the lyrical and visceral dimensions of human experience that arise from a direct engagement with nature. Fallingwater echoes nineteenth-century attitudes advanced by Emerson, Whitman, Wordsworth, Thoreau, Lowell, Ruskin, and Morris, among others who, like Frederick Law Olmsted, called for in an almost religious tone the necessity of interacting "with environments where nature remained dominant, even if transformed in some measure through art or other human agency."[1] Nature's sublimity as depicted on mid-nineteenth-century American landscape canvases offered a foundation from which a morally redemptive ethos would emerge and seize the imaginations of philosophers, writers, artists, and social critics as a means to counter the excesses of industrial society. One can imagine in Thomas Cole's *Essay on American Scenery* (1836) a prefiguring of Wright's romantic vision for Fallingwater and its inhabitants, which would occur one hundred years later, when he wrote of trees in a way suggestive of a new ennobled human social condition, free from cultural influence, and made possible only through an encounter with the forces of nature and wild things.

"Trees are like men, differing widely in character, in sheltered spots or under the influence of culture, they show few contrasting points; peculiarities are pruned and trained away, until there is a general resemblance. But in exposed situations, wild and uncultivated, battling with the elements and with one another for some morsel of soil, or a favoring rock to which they may cling—they exhibit striking peculiarities, and sometimes grand originality."[2]

Wright's "ethical valorization of nature"[3] as embodied at Fallingwater diverged from mainstream International Style Modernism, and persists today not only through its dramatic intersection with its site but also through its harmonious affinity with nature, its cycles and rhythms, systems and forces. Integrated intimately with nature, Fallingwater continues to point the way forward toward realizing a sustainable ethos in the way it allows us to dwell. As pointed out by Karsten Harries, Martin Heidegger's notion of dwelling—derived from the Old English and German term for building, *buan*, itself derived from the root word *bauen* or "being"—implies not only an intimate relationship with one's surroundings but also one of cultivation, meaning "at the same time to cherish and protect, to preserve and care for."[4] Harries expresses the cultivation analogy in words that recall Edgar Kaufmann jr.'s claim that harmony with nature is necessary for the very existence of mankind, arguing that "we must cultivate also, not just the soil, but land, water, and air, cultivate this fragile earth, cultivation that should take care that what remains the indispensable ground of human dwelling will not be destroyed by our greed, our will to power, or perhaps just our

thoughtlessness."[5] Fallingwater manifests Harries's call to action that architecture, like pre-modern agriculture, should, be such an through acts of cultivation, reclaim its status as a 'tending' and sustainable profession.

Toward a Path of Resistance: Fallingwater and the Modern Movement

Fallingwater's profound accord with nature and its capacity to advance architecture as an act of cultivation differed in effect from the work of many European practitioners of the modernist aesthetic whose architecture expressed a separation between humankind and nature. For architects Le Corbusier and Mies van der Rohe, among the foremost proponents of this aesthetic, architecture's relationship to landscape was predominately scenographic, where the land and its elements remain intact, distinct, and decidedly removed from intimate human encounter. Le Corbusier articulated this detachment as he described the setting of his iconic image of the machine age, the Villa Savoye (1929–31): "The site: a spreading grassy meadow in the shape of a flattened dome . . . the house . . . a box hovering in the air . . . in the midst of fields overlooking the orchard. . . . The occupants . . . found this rural setting beautiful . . . who came here because they will contemplate it in its preserved state from the top of their roof garden or through their long windows facing in all directions. Their home life will be enfolded in a Virgilian Dream."[6]

It is the roof garden at Le Corbusier's Villa Savoye that becomes the metaphorical landscape, a replacement for the ground plane and location from which one is offered what William Curtis has described as "vignettes of super-real intensity over the grass and trees."[7] The roof garden caps Le Corbusier's section type elucidated by his five points, the organizational ideology that situates circulation and service spaces below, major living spaces at mid-section, and his "arcadia imagined" at the roof level. As a lens into nature, Villa Savoye's roof-as-idealized-landscape and its emphasis on visual content reformulates landscape experience into an ethereal construction of wind, sun, and sky that appeals to the intellect in a way that markedly contrasts Wright's intensely sensual, terrestrial experience at Fallingwater.

At the Farnsworth House (1946–50), Mies van der Rohe advanced a more philosophical, aesthetically inclined attitude aimed at creating an idealized unity between humanity, nature, and architecture when he stated: "Indeed we should strive to bring Nature, houses and people together in greater unity. When one looks at nature through the glass walls of the Farnsworth House it takes on a deeper significance than when one stands outside. More of nature is thus expressed— it becomes part of a greater whole."[8] For Mies, direct engagement with the land diminished its aesthetic pleasure. Instead, he encouraged human confrontation with the landscape in the form of an active spectator who constructs the setting's pictorial character through selectively limiting its scenery as in the experience of landscape painting. Mies further argued that nature's palimpsest should remain predominantly free from traces of human activity that could encumber or disturb its unalloyed character.

At the elevated, temple-like Farnsworth House, Mies's relationship to nature remains at a distance through his choreography of carefully framed views. Separated from nature and its elements by a thin peripteral glass skin at Farnsworth House, one discovers its essence at a remove, as an intellectually constructed place. This is in contrast to the non-idealized tactile experiences offered by Wright who at Fallingwater invites us to *discover* place as we are subsumed into, and become one with, nature.

Wright and Aalto as Modern Eclectics: Heterotopia at Fallingwater and Villa Mairea

And this is the task of the house: to reveal the world, not as essence but as presence, that is, as material and color, topography and vegetation, seasons, weather and light.
—Christian Norberg-Schulz

Christian Norberg-Schulz's assertion that the house is the primary vehicle through which one experiences his being part of the world occurs through engagement with the sensual presence of phenomena, not as an intellectually constructed essence. This presence is accomplished through the house's capacity to *keep* and *visualize* phenomena, making them accessible to the inhabitant as a means to experience and interpret their world. Wright's Fallingwater and Alvar Aalto's Villa Mairea evoke the spirit of their respective settings through their encounter with phenomena and site-specific tectonic expression. Both resist the modernist tendency toward what Demetri Porphyrios refers to as *homotopia* or the "state of mind where differences are put aside and expansive unities are established favoring continuity, familiarity, and recurrence."[9] Porphyrios notes this condition in the universalizing grids of Mies van der Rohe where, for example at Crown Hall, "by gridding space, one safeguarded against all accidents or indiscreet intrusions, and established instead an idealized field of likeness."[10] Conversely, Fallingwater and Villa Mairea, in response to their settings, approach the spatial condition of heterotopia or "that peculiar sense of order where fragments of a number of possible coherences glitter separately."[11] While Fallingwater's implied spatial tartan and Villa Mairea's structural articulation of its major living spaces make reference to the grid, the grid's propensity to dominate is carefully mediated through the heterotopic or varied disposition of major architectural elements in each of their plans and their intersection with site phenomena, often realized through the dramatic use of diagonal movement.

Aalto had a profound admiration for Wright and for Fallingwater and was deeply influenced by Wright's 1938 Museum of Modern Art exhibition in New York and Fallingwater's publication in the American popular media, eventually visiting the Kaufmanns at Bear Run in 1940. In his early proposals for Villa Mairea (1938–39), Aalto actually proposed that the owners, Harry and Maire Gullichsen, build over a waterfall on land originally owned by Maire's grandfather. Although the Gullichsens did not pursue the idea, Aalto's early sketches were heavily influenced by Fallingwater, including dramatic cantilevered balconies over a free-form first level that served as a metaphor for Fallingwater's natural stream condition.[12] In subsequent schemes, the free forms of the first level would find expression in Maire's studio on the second level, but the teak-clad living room and upper terrace balcony's connection to Fallingwater remains clear. Like Fallingwater, Villa Mairea is based upon a series of squares in plan with vivid diagonal sequences. At Fallingwater, a striking diagonal experience links the compressed entry with the sunlit west terrace in a way that suggests

movement from cave to bower, or refuge to prospect. A second diagonal relates the fireplace to the horizontal triple-sash opening to Bear Run below or, as Neil Levine points out, from fire to water. At Villa Mairea, a major diagonal reinforced by the angle of the low wall that separates the entrance hall from the dining room connects the living room entry to the fireplace. Within the large square that contains the villa's more public living spaces, a second pair of diagonals establishes connections between the main stair with the southwest corner and its views to the expansive lawn and approach to the villa, while a second links the private study to the winter garden with views to the northwest and courtyard. Beyond their diagonal planning, it is the sensuous tectonic expression found in architectural elements in the living rooms at Fallingwater and Villa Mairea—such as the fireplace with its boulder-strewn hearth and flagstone floor, hatch to Bear Run, and Edgar Kaufmann's library at Fallingwater and the main stair, fireplace, steel-clad columns, pine-strip ceiling, and multiple floor materials at Villa Mairea—that advances each house's heterotopic spatial reading while eliciting vibrant natural associations. Memories of caves and rock ledges at Fallingwater and the experience of the Nordic forest at Villa Mairea are brought to life through these architectural elements as they engage each site's topography, materiality, phenomena, and seasonal change, uniquely experienced through movement in space.

Site Specificity and Place Formation at Fallingwater

> *A building has one site. In this one situation, its intentions are collected. Building and Site have been interdependent since the beginning of Architecture. In the past, this connection was manifest without conscious intention through the use of local materials and craft, and by an association with events of history and myth. Today the link between site and architecture must be found in new ways, which are a part of a constructive transformation in modern life.*
> —Steven Holl

Architect Steven Holl argues, "Architecture's meaning lies in the intertwining of its site, its phenomena, its idea."[13] Fallingwater's anchoring results from the unique site-specific relationships that emerge from the intertwining of these three elements that situate architecture as a "place form" and a foundation for the creation of sustainabe environments. Fallingwater's experience begins with the landscape and the building approach that anticipates and reveals the formal and material nature of the yet-to-be-experienced house. En route to the house, one experiences the rich and varied vegetation including the flowering rhododendron, whose leaf's underside will determine the light peach color of Fallingwater's concrete elements. Beneath the rhododendron, layers of variegated Pottsville sandstone quarried on site through the aid of local labor establish its formal appearance and material identity. Robert McCarter points out that Fallingwater's connection to the site's rock ledges is particularly lucid in winter when roofs and terraces are draped in snow, rendering it nearly indistinguishable from the waterfall's rock layers. He also notes that the stone ledges act as a mnemonic device that recall the rock cliffs of Wright's native Wisconsin and their representation at Taliesin.[14] Situated above the falls, the initial encounter with Fallingwater reveals both its phenomena and idea. The sound of the water emanating from the still-concealed falls and the dappled light and shadow that play on the "floating" south-facing terraces establish Fallingwater's cantilevered idea, prefigured by Wright in his earliest perspective sketch. There, Wright's notion that one must "start with the ground"[15] and begin "there where they stand"[16] is crystallized, implying that "in any and every case the character of the site is the beginning of the building that aspires to architecture."[17] In a related observation akin to Olmsted, Kenneth Frampton speaks of a total metaphysical fusion with site that is predominantly achieved from the effect of Fallingwater's stone and water, noting "[t]hat the rough stone walls and flagged floors intend some primitive homage to the site is borne out by the living room stairs which, descending through the floor to the waterfall below, have no function other than to bring man into more intimate communion with the surface of the stream."[18] This metaphysical site fusion is further emphasized when the descending stair, constructed as a filigree of thin concrete treads and lightweight vertical steel supports, is juxtaposed in direct opposition to the stone stairs ascending to the second and third levels. McCarter suggests the contrasting tectonic character of the stairs creates a "gravitational reversal" activated by the seemingly lightweight stair penetrating the stone floor to float over the water and the "heavy" stone stair rising two floors to emerge at the level of the treetops.[19] Defying traditional conceptions of visual weight and support, this reversal establishes an inimitable, dynamic equilibrium with the site. Extended observation yields yet a deeper, primordial awareness of the site through Fallingwater's commingling with the four elements. Earth and water appear literally and metaphorically in the polished flagstone floor and the hearth's emerging unpolished boulder that recalls the stream below. Air and fire resonate in the aerie-like sensation of the terraces and the massive fireplace. The interplay of site-forces and architectural elements metaphorically and physically anchors Fallingwater to its site taking it beyond architecture to a "place form" condition that is both enduring and an exemplary model for the cause of an architectural sustainability that begins with the intertwining of site, its "idea," and phenomena.

Fallingwater as Integrated Architecture: The Organic Metaphor and Assisted Nature

> It is the nature of any organic building to grow from its site, come out of the ground into the light—the ground itself held always as a basic part of the building itself . . . . A building dignified as a tree in the midst of nature . . . . But instead of "organic" we might say "natural" building. Or we might say integral building.
> —Frank Lloyd Wright

Frank Lloyd Wright called his architecture "organic" to distinguish it from what he called the "pseudoclassic order of the schools, derived mainly from grafted attempts at reclassification called the 'International Style.'"[20] In Wright's view, architecture is organic when it becomes intrinsic in such a way that it "cultivates 'the space within' as a reality instead of the roof and walls: it is building from inside out, instead of outside in."[21] Derived naturally from the inside out, organic architecture and the land meet symbiotically, becoming "more essential to the other"[22] as they meld into one entity: *landscape*. This architecture-landscape amalgam infers that organic architecture is analogous

to natural form—concerned with the integrity of nature's innate structure—and beyond style, becoming Wright's response to "the demand of our modern American life for a higher spiritual order."[23] Wright's vision repeatedly stresses that the architectural features of the "democratic plan" should rise naturally from the topography, taking on the character of the ground and becoming an *integral* part—an organic feature of the ground, "according to place and purpose."[24]

One of the organic metaphors often cited by Wright, the tree presents living architectural lessons through its shifting qualities of light and shadow, its prospect as shelter of varied intensity and enclosure, and its contrasting deep-rootedness and natural expansion. Catherine Howett characterizes this expansion dynamically, noting that the tree extends "outward toward the enveloping sky—literally breathing to the pulse of dynamic systems tied to the earth and the air."[25] In this way organic architecture at Fallingwater portends a proto-sustainability or form of *assisted nature*, using modest architectural means to accommodate and be assimilated within, rather than simulate or control, natural environmental patterns and processes. Clearly many sustainable trajectories are evident at Fallingwater that respond to the site's natural forces. The south-facing terraces afford stunning inside-outside relationships and distinct vantage to the experience of Bear Run and the surrounding forest as they respond to the cyclical patterns of the sun, facilitating natural ventilation and illumination. Through their overhangs and supporting trellises, the upper terraces provide appropriate sun protection to the lower levels and their wide expanses of horizontal glazing. The hatch to Bear Run serves as a thermal siphon drawing cool air up from Bear Run during the day, reversing the process at night. Wright's use of locally quarried stone and site-manufactured concrete, in addition to their strong site-specific and aesthetic outcomes, substantially reduced the building's environmental footprint. While not entirely without continuing technical challenges, nor completely sustainable when measured from the contemporary LEED standard, Fallingwater's organic affinity with the site offers something much more—a profound respect for nature and its elements that finds translation through Wright's architectural response and an affection for the land and the place engendered in those who experience it. Fallingwater's tectonics reveal its site and the nature of its making at a visceral level. Peter Bohlin, architect of the lyrical Ledge House (1996), himself a romantic modernist, argues that creating emotionally resonant places that people will value and love, like Fallingwater, is "one of the most sustainable building practices."[26] Fallingwater remains the most memorable of these places.

Fallingwater's Enduring Legacy and Promise

> *To Wright, architecture was a great inclusive agency through which humankind adapted the environment to human needs and, reciprocally, attuned life to the cosmos; amid continual changes architecture could keep human life more natural and nature more humane.*
> —Edgar Kaufmann jr.

Fallingwater's legacy endures in the timeless statement it makes about life in harmony with nature made vividly apparent through Wright's total integration of architecture and site. Wright's architectural vision, while grounded in the nineteenth century, informed both American and international architectural trajectories throughout the twentieth century, and its echoes resound within the current debates shaping contemporary architecture's prospect to advance the causes of sustainability and environmental stewardship. Although sharing their utopian optimism about the liberating role of the machine in twentieth-century life, Wright chose a path markedly different from most of his European modernist colleagues when he pursued a more dynamic and terrestrial rapport with nature and site. Fallingwater's anchored relationship with the site at both a physical and metaphysical level situates it uniquely among the iconic examples of the heroic period of the modern movement. Fallingwater firmly moved beyond a "scenography of site" to establish an instinctually sensual and humanely sustainable connection with its setting at Bear Run.

In so doing, Wright adapted the environment to human needs with a footprint that, while legible, heightens the experience of the site, extending its meaning like a palimpsest, evident in the way that Fallingwater gently overwrites its site patterns, humanizing them, allowing us to become, as Edgar Kaufmann suggests, "more natural." The consequence of becoming "more natural" or "at one with nature," cannot be underestimated as it has, and will continue to influence, how generations of architects view the land. With a cogency that can be likened to conservationist Aldo Leopold's simple, poetic strain "When we see land as a community to which we belong, we may begin to use it with love and respect,"[27] Fallingwater can be envisioned as nature's agent, its advocate. Wright, like Leopold, understood that nature as community includes the soil, water, fauna, and flora conjoined to its human inhabitants, as the raw materials of wilderness become the building blocks of civilization.

Nobly responding to land and nature's cyclical circumstances and mysteries, Fallingwater remains a dream-like place where memories born of one's encounter with nature resound life-long. Its lessons unfold slowly as if in song, inviting all to participate "each singing what belongs to him or her, and to none else."[28] Liliane Kaufmann perhaps expressed this sentiment best as she confided to Wright: "Living in a house built by you has been my one education."[29] Fallingwater's lessons will continue to persist in their legacy and promise, occupying the mind's eye of all who believe that architecture can reassert its role as a *tending* profession and promote the advancement of human experience and environmental quality—as it continues to touch, as suggested by Paul Rudolf, "something deep within us, about which, finally, none of us can speak."

STRENGTHENING FALLINGWATER

By Robert Silman

On a quiet day in the summer of 1995 our office receptionist informed me that Lynda Waggoner, director of Fallingwater, was on the telephone. Lynda described the ongoing problem with cracking of the concrete parapets on the master bedroom terrace. She asked if we would be interested in coming out to take a look.

How could we say no? This, after all, was the number one building in the whole United States, voted the best all-time work of American architecture by the American Institute of Architects (AIA). Although the entire professions of architecture, engineering, and historic preservation would be following our every move, we relished the challenge and of course responded with an emphatic yes.

Our first site visit confirmed the suspicions. In a building of this age, cracks, once repaired, were not supposed to open at the same location each time they had been patched. Yet anecdotal evidence showed that the cantilevers were continuing to deflect. The top sides of the cantilever beams, at the point of maximum stress, were cracking and, even after being repaired and painted over, were cracking again at the same locations. The building was apparently moving.

Our first step was to monitor the building accurately in order to determine definitively that there was a long-term trend towards continuing deflection. So far, all that we had was subjective evidence.

First, there was the story of the removal of the formwork in 1935, after the concrete had gained sufficient strength to stand on its own. When Wright's on-site apprentice, Bob Mosher, witnessed the removal of the last prop under the cantilever of the living room he, like everyone else there, became alarmed when the entire structure deflected about 1¾ inches. Although this immediate deflection was easily predictable by advance calculations, apparently no one had thought to camber the formwork for the concrete upward by at least that amount so when it did deflect, the structure would come back to the level position. In addition, cracks opened in the master bedroom terrace concrete parapet beams. Bob Mosher immediately telephoned back to Wright's studio at Taliesin in Spring Green, Wisconsin, reporting the deflection and cracks; they in turn called the principal structural engineer, Mendel Glickman, in Madison. Glickman is reported to have asked for a moment to check his calculations and the drawings. Then he came back to the phone and said, "Oh my God, I forgot the negative reinforcing!" The negative reinforcing that he referred to would have been steel reinforcing bars placed in the top of the master bedroom terrace–level beams running north-south on each edge of the terrace. Instead, only very small, very short bars were placed here.

Knowing of that supposed interchange in 1935, we still needed to know about the history of the movements in the house from that time until the present. Our measurements at the site indicated that at some locations the main floor cantilever had deflected nearly 7 inches with respect to the support point of the cantilever some fifteen feet away. The master bedroom terrace had deflected similarly. These numbers were extremely large, more than ten to fifteen times what we would normally design for.

Checking through the archives at Fallingwater, we found that Edgar Kaufmann Sr. seemed to be only moderately concerned with these movements and cracks. Between the time that the

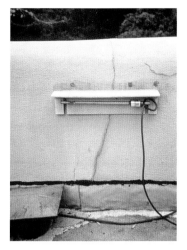

fig. 1

page 260: View looking southwest, upwards, toward strengthened terraces from below falls of Bear Run.

fig. 1: View of terrace wall showing cracks prior to strengthening and restoration. *Western Pennsylvania Conservancy.*

house was completed in 1937 and 1945, he only had the deflections surveyed once. Thereafter until his death in 1955 he commissioned 16 visits by the surveyor. We could find no record of Edgar Kaufmann jr. ever commissioning such a survey after his father's death. Instead, he asked the chief of maintenance, Earl Friend, to keep his eye on things. Earl's method was simple: the first time he measured he cut a length of wood to fit exactly between the master bedroom terrace–level and the main-level parapets. Each time he went back to check—by inserting the wood in the same spot—there was no change. Of course what Earl did not realize was that the two cantilevers were moving together and were not changing relative to one another but were deflecting at the same rate!

Thus we discounted all previous surveys and designed a high-tech electronic monitoring system that would give us information on very small movements that could be recorded on a data-logger and downloaded onto a computer. Over a seventeen-month period, we found, as expected, that there was a definite trend toward ongoing downward deflection of the cantilevers.

How could this be? Reinforced concrete seems about as solid a material as one could want for building a house. It is likely that Edgar Kaufmann Sr. and jr. both agreed with this sentiment, even though they were aware that the house was still cracking each time they repaired it. But as engineers, we know that many solids, such as concrete, exhibit small movements under continuous loads, a phenomenon called plastic flow or "creep." The continuous load here is the heavy weight of the concrete house itself. In general we say that 90% of the plastic flow occurs in the first year after casting, and the remaining 10% continues in a gradually reducing quantity for about twenty years more until it ceases to move. But the house was now almost sixty years old and was still experiencing plastic flow. To an engineer this was very scary. It is almost never seen in an existing building and, ultimately, is an indication of impending failure.

During the seventeen months of monitoring, we also made calculations of the actual stresses and strains in the reinforced concrete of the structure. We could calculate the loads quite easily, and we knew the dimensions of all the members from the original drawings that we verified with site observations. One thing that we noticed in the original drawings was that the south end of the master bedroom terrace was shown to be supported on four very small structural steel T-shaped members, continuing below in the south wall of the living room. When we looked out the living room windows to the south, we saw that four of the mullions were larger, corresponding to the locations of the steel T-shaped supports. We removed a metal covering at one of these larger mullions and verified that it indeed contained a support of the dimension called for in the drawings. This confirmed our suspicion that Earl's measurements using the cut piece of wood were not meaningful. In addition, it caused us to shift our focus from the master bedroom terrace parapet beams where the cracking was most obvious to the main floor cantilever girders that were, in the end, supporting not only the main floor but also the master bedroom terrace.

The major stumbling block for our analysis occurred in trying to determine the amount of reinforcing in the main floor concrete girders. Once again the archives proved to be essential. A memo from Bob Mosher to Mr. Wright sent four days after the concrete for the living room and the terraces was poured stated, "I am enclosing some calculations made in Pittsburgh by engineers hired by Kaufmann: their contention was that more steel [was] necessary in beams because they discovered that the weight of [the] second floor transposed through T-iron window frames was not figured. Steel was sent out and put in at last moment. Our builder does not trust us . . ." Mr. Wright's response to Mr. Kaufmann is one of the classics of the architect-client relationship. "If you are paying to have the concrete engineering done down there, there is no use whatever in our doing it here. I am willing you should take it over but I am not willing to be insulted. So we will send no more steel diagrams. I am unaccustomed to such treatment where I have built buildings before and do not intend to put up with it now . . . I don't know what kind of architect you are familiar with but it apparently isn't the kind I think I am. You seem not to know how to treat a decent one. I have put so much more into this house than you or any other client has a right to expect that if I haven't your confidence—to hell with the whole thing."

The archives also revealed a report commissioned by Mr. Kaufmann nine months later from the firm of Pittsburgh engineers that Bob Mosher had referred to—Metzger-Richardson Co., Engineers & Fabricators, Steel for Concrete—stating that they had installed twice the amount of reinforcing in the main living room girders as had been shown on the original design drawings. They calculated the stresses in the concrete and the steel at the main floor girders and concluded, "These stresses are not satisfactory. . . . [They] do not fall within the limits of those prescribed by accepted engineering practice. [T]herefore the structure does not have a satisfactory factor of safety, or what might be termed reserve strength."

We felt that it was crucial that we determine the exact amount of reinforcing steel in these girders. Although we had not yet prepared calculations, our instincts warned us that the stresses were very high in the concrete girders and we dared not cut into them significantly to expose the reinforcement. Any diminution of strength was a potential source of disaster. Instead we decided to use a technique called non-destructive evaluation in which a specialty contractor uses tools such as impulse radar and magnetic detection to find actual quantities, sizes and locations of reinforcing bars hidden in concrete. Their results confirmed that Metzger-Richardson had indeed inserted the extra bars referred to in their report.

At several locations where the levels of stress were not high, we recovered samples of the concrete and reinforcing steel and sent them to a laboratory for testing. The concrete proved to be of excellent quality. Although it was hand mixed on the job site using local aggregate, the ultimate compressive strength tested out at more than 5,000 psi (pounds per square inch), 50% more than anticipated. And the reinforcing met the chemical and physical requirements typical of steel for that period. We were now ready to accomplish the task of calculating the stresses in the actual structure. The tools available to us in the late 1990s were far more advanced than those in Mendel Glickman's arsenal in 1935. We utilized sophisticated computer programs using finite element methods and three-dimensional modeling that gave very accurate results for both stresses and movements of the structure. We were able to compare the calculated movements with the actual observed movements in the structure and then fine-tune the computer model until the two agreed. In the end, we found that the beams in the parapets of the master bedroom terrace were not able to carry any significant load (remember that the negative reinforcing had been omitted by mistake); all of the load of both the master bedroom terrace and the main level was being carried in the four main girders under the living room floor. It was these girders to which Metzger and Richardson had added reinforcing, but alas, they had not added enough. The easternmost of the four girders was supported on a slender steel post that was part of the stair going down to the stream below, so this member was not overstressed. However the other three girders showed alarming results. Both the concrete and the reinforcing steel were stressed way beyond their allowable limits—the former to 95% of its failure strength and the latter beyond its elastic limit. Normally we would limit these stresses to one-half or two-thirds of these values. In all of our years of practice, we had never seen an active, working building with such high levels of stress. All of the safety factors had been wiped out!

In 1935 the principles of reinforced concrete design were well known; every engineering student could calculate the required reinforcement in a cantilever beam. Mendel Glickman, Wes Peters, and Metzger-Richardson were all accomplished engineers. How could they have missed this?

One explanation for the error in the original design might be the speed at which Fallingwater was designed. After Mr. Wright's initial visit to the site several months elapsed, and Mr. Kaufmann had heard nothing. According to a tale that I heard personally related several times during the 1990s by Edgar Tafel, the lead design apprentice on the house, Mr. Kaufmann called Taliesin early one morning to inform Mr. Wright that he was in Milwaukee and was going to drive over to Spring Green to look at the plans. Mr. Wright heartily invited him, saying that they would lunch together and after that they would go over the drawings.

Now at this time there was not yet a line on paper. Mr. Wright gathered the apprentices around him, overlaid the site survey with a piece of tracing paper, and began to draw. First, the foundation plan showing the bolsters, then the main floor, then the second floor with the master bedroom and terrace, then the third floor. As he finished, the butler announced Mr. Kaufmann's arrival and Mr. Wright hurriedly showed the apprentices what he wanted the elevations to look like, charging them to draw these during lunch.

When they came back to the studio after lunch Mr. Kaufmann was reportedly thrilled with the scheme that Mr. Wright showed him and wanted to start construction immediately. Thus the working drawings, including the calculations for the reinforcing steel in the concrete must have been produced exceedingly quickly. It is very possible that Glickman and Peters showed some reinforcing bars in the main floor girders as a "place holder," fully intending to go back later and perform a final design. But perhaps in the rush to get the drawings out to the contractor in the field, this got overlooked.

We cannot, however, imagine why Metzger-Richardson did not supply the correct amount of steel when they increased the number of bars to twice the amount shown on the design drawings. Perhaps they too did not have time to perform an accurate calculation and were acting on instinct. When they went back nine months later and did precise calculations, they realized that the steel that they had put in was not adequate.

However, even armed with this information, Mr. Kaufmann elected to believe Mr. Wright that the house was perfectly safe for occupancy, for he never acted on any of the suggestions made by Metzger-Richardson to reduce the length of the cantilevers.

Immediately upon learning the results of our calculations, we notified Ms. Waggoner. Distressed

fig. 3

and worried, she conveyed the information to the advisory committee. They shot back the crucial questions: Is the building safe? Can we continue to allow visitors and staff to enter into it?

The answers were not clear. The structure was no different from what it had been on day one of its existence. Its problems had nothing to do with aging, deterioration, corrosion, breakdown of the concrete, or stress due to occupancy loads. There was simply insufficient reinforcing in the three concrete girders in the living room floor—a deficiency had been built into the original structure.

In the end we did not answer their questions directly but rather convinced the advisory committee to agree to repair the problem, whatever it took. We then stated that, if they were going to undertake a repair campaign, we would need to shore the three concrete girders temporarily, so why not shore them immediately, even before we had decided on a repair scheme? They agreed, and a single line of shoring was installed under the cantilevers in 1997.

Even the shoring required an intricate design and installation. The stream had to be temporarily diverted, holes for anchor bolts carefully drilled into the stream's bedrock floor, the rock overhang of the waterfall temporarily shored up, and then the line of steel shoring erected.

While the shoring was being installed on site, we were working in the office to develop repair schemes. Even before we had established the full scope of the problem and completed the calculations, we had been thinking about possible alternative repair solutions. Several universities assigned the problem in their classes. Solutions came from all over the country, and we were ready to listen to anything that seemed a remote possibility.

One obvious choice was to strengthen the deficient concrete girders with new structural steel "sister" members that would be placed on each side of each girder. This would have required much more temporary shoring as each of the 4-inch-wide concrete joists would have to be cut free from the existing girders in order to install the sisters. Then the joists would have to be reconnected. This solution would do nothing to correct the existing level of stress in the concrete or the steel reinforcing bars. It would merely transfer the entire load onto the new sister girders.

Another solution would be to bond reinforcing plates made either of carbon fiber or steel to

fig. 3: View of temporary shoring beneath living room cantilever. Photo by Robert P. Ruschak. *Western Pennsylvania Conservancy.*

the top sides of the girders using epoxy adhesive, once the floor had been removed. If these could be made thin enough, then they could be buried in the eventual built-up finished flooring installation. This solution, too, did nothing to remedy the existing high level of stress.

Finally some hard-core preservationists suggested that in accordance with the strictest principles of historic preservation, no existing historic fabric be removed or disturbed and the shoring be left in place permanently. The reasons for such a solution would be explained to visitors and would be in any text that accompanied pictures of the stabilized structure.

But we were not happy with any of these proposed solutions. What our office envisioned was a fix that would not alter Fallingwater's unusual beauty, would retain the principle of the cantilever, and would utilize the existing concrete as much as possible.

Our office ultimately developed a repair scheme using a technique called post-tensioned concrete. In this procedure, very high-strength steel cables would be installed adjacent to both sides of each concrete girder. The cables would be placed in an inverted V configuration, anchored into a new block of concrete located some fifteen feet north of the supports for the girders, sloped over a diverter block at the support point, and threaded through a temporary hole cut into the south parapet wall. In order to install the tendons to their proper slope, a series of 4-inch-diameter holes would be drilled into the concrete joists, but otherwise the joists would remain fully attached to the girders. These cables or tendons would then be inserted into a hollow plastic tube and would be free to move during the construction phase.

Once all of the tendons were in place and anchored, a high-capacity hydraulic jack would be attached to the cables outside the south parapet, on temporary scaffolding rising up from the stream, and the tendons pulled with an enormous force—up to 390 tons in each girder. The tendons would then be wedged tight and permanently locked off to an anchorage block just beneath the surface of the face of the south parapet. The jacks could then be removed without losing the tension in the cables. The large tensile force in the cables induces an equally large and opposite compression force in the girders. Because the tendons are not horizontal but are rather sloped to a very carefully calculated alignment, the stress imparted to the existing girders actually reduces the existing very high compression in the concrete and tension in the reinforcing bars by introducing reverse forces. This solution required the least amount of intervention, was the only one that significantly reduced the existing overstresses, and was, in the end, the most cost-effective by far. Our projected schedule showed that the work could be accomplished over the winter when the house traditionally closes.

All of the work would be done from the top side of the slab, after the finished floor had been carefully removed. This would allow the work to proceed in all weather. Materials and manpower could be delivered from the exterior directly into the south end of the living room via the temporary scaffold built up from the streambed and concrete pumped from trucks parked on the other side of the stream. Repairs began in November 2001 and the house reopened on schedule in April 2002, a period of less than six months. There was no loss of a visitor season because of repairs.

In order to ensure that our solution was indeed the best possible one, we counseled the advisory committee to conduct a peer review among leading specialists in concrete and historic preservation throughout the world. The peer reviewers had several months to study our proposed solution and

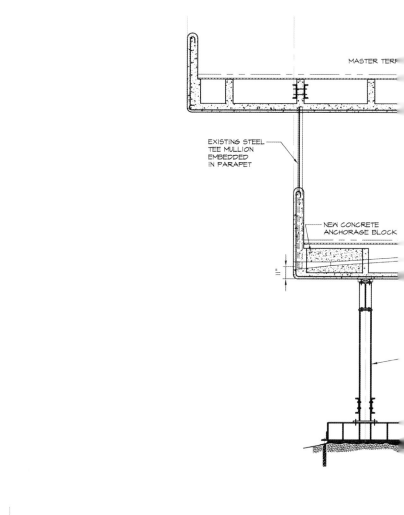

MASTER TERF

EXISTING STEEL
TEE MULLION
EMBEDDED
IN PARAPET

NEW CONCRETE
ANCHORAGE BLOCK

1"

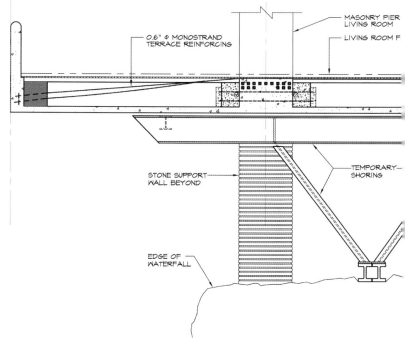

MASONRY PIER
LIVING ROOM

LIVING ROOM F

0.6" Φ MONOSTRAND
TERRACE REINFORCING

TEMPORARY
SHORING

STONE SUPPORT
WALL BEYOND

EDGE OF
WATERFALL

fig. 4: Building sections diagramming the realized plan to use post-tensioned concrete for structural repairs to the master bedroom terrace, living room, and east and west terraces off of living room. Repairs involved relieving the stresses in the cantilever beams through the creative use of post-tensioning cables. The tension in the cables acts to exert a positive force to counteract the negative force caused by cantilever action.

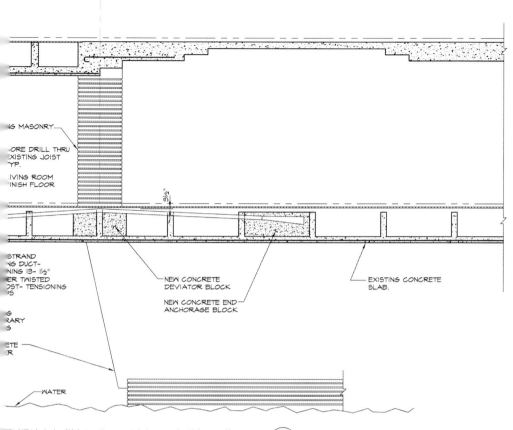

NG MASONRY

ORE DRILL THRU
EXISTING JOIST
YP.

IVING ROOM
INISH FLOOR

3½"

STRAND
NG DUCT-
NING 13- 1½"
ER TWISTED
OST- TENSIONING
S

G
RARY
S

ETE
R

WATER

NEW CONCRETE
DEVIATOR BLOCK

NEW CONCRETE END
ANCHORAGE BLOCK

EXISTING CONCRETE
SLAB.

THRU LIVING ROOM LOOKING WEST   (1 / S-4)

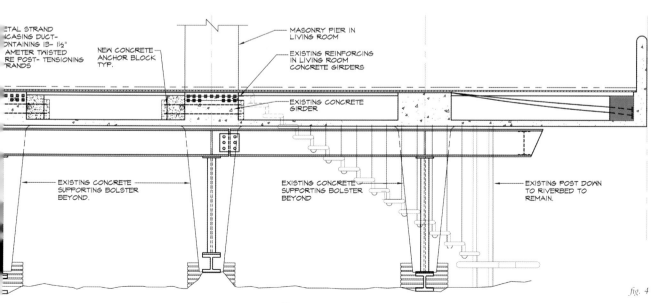

ETAL STRAND
NCASING DUCT-
ONTAINING 13- 1½"
AMETER TWISTED
RE POST- TENSIONING
TRANDS

NEW CONCRETE
ANCHOR BLOCK
TYP.

MASONRY PIER IN
LIVING ROOM

EXISTING REINFORCING
IN LIVING ROOM
CONCRETE GIRDERS

EXISTING CONCRETE
GIRDER

EXISTING CONCRETE
SUPPORTING BOLSTER
BEYOND.

EXISTING CONCRETE
SUPPORTING BOLSTER
BEYOND

EXISTING POST DOWN
TO RIVERBED TO
REMAIN.

fig. 4

THRU LIVING ROOM LOOKING NORTH   (2 / S-4)

they presented their findings to a standing room–only audience in the Carnegie Museum of Art in Pittsburgh. They strongly endorsed the proposed repair as the most cost-effective and appropriate to the needs of the property.

The contractor selected to make the concrete repairs was VSL of Springfield, Virginia, a contractor specializing in post-tensioning. Their affiliated firm, Structural Preservation Systems of Baltimore, Maryland, assisted with concrete repairs.

Moving forward, the first step was to remove all the built-in furniture. Then the maintenance staff of Fallingwater carefully removed each of the stones from the finished floor, numbered them, and recorded their exact position. They were stored on site in temporary shelters. The existing wooden subfloor and its 2x4 wood purlins were removed and discarded. Removal of the stone flooring had been achieved previously by the maintenance staff in order to install new waterproofing on the terraces, so they were confident that this could be accomplished without incident.

Our office had prepared the initial calculations. We then retained a consultant who specialized in post-tensioning, Schupack Suarez/TDEG, with Mario Suarez leading their team. They verified and refined our calculation. VSL then made a third set of calculations to be sure that the geometry and the stresses were correct before they proceeded with the work.

The dead-end anchor blocks, central diverter blocks, and jacking-end anchorage blocks of concrete were first poured and clamped to each existing girder. On each side of two of the girders, wire bundles—composed of thirteen strands of 1/2-inch-diameter twisted steel wire—were threaded through the hollow tube and anchored to the dead-end block. At the easternmost girder to be reinforced, the bundle could only be placed on one side because of the presence of the stair going down to the stream; thus only 10 strands were placed on one side of this girder.

The worst deflection was noted at the tips of the east and west terraces, which are double cantilevers. The main girders were cantilevered in the north-south direction and the terrace cantilevered off of these in the east-west direction. We found it prudent to reduce the stresses in the terrace cantilevers as well and to do this we used smaller post-tensioning cables called monostrand. These were installed in advance of the post-tensioning of the main girders.

Each of the 1/2-inch diameter strands had a working strength capability of 40,000 pounds of tension. Calculations required that we use thirteen strands in a bundle on each side of the two western girders, one girder carrying a force of 780,000 pounds and the other 858,800 pounds. The remaining easternmost girder's ten strands carried a force of 330,400 pounds.

On a very pleasant day in February 2002, I flew to Pittsburgh with John Matteo, our project manager, and then drove to Fallingwater. On the drive, I felt myself growing anxious. I had recently finished a four-month tour working the twelve-hour night shift once a week at the World Trade Center site, helping the first responders place heavy equipment and evaluate stability of existing roadways, makeshift ramps, and access paths. The memory of whistles blowing while work stopped and a dead hero's body was lifted from the wreckage brought tears to my eyes, as it still does.

Then there was the worry of what we were about to attempt at Fallingwater. Post-tensioning had not been commonly used for making repairs to severely distressed concrete buildings. What if there were some obscure forces that we had not accounted for in our calculations? Might the application of the huge jacking force cause the concrete, already stressed to 95% of its capacity, to rupture? We had installed some shoring towers within the living room just in case. Still, I was worried.

The next morning, we began the delicate post-tensioning operation. Tension force was to be introduced in three stages. The first stage would be 20% of the force, sufficient to set the tendons. Then an additional 30% would be added and this was to be left overnight. Measurements were taken to record forces in the tendons as well as movements in the girders. Strain gauges in the four steel T-shaped supports at the south parapet indicated that there were unequal forces being transmitted up to the master bedroom terrace. In order to verify this reading, Mario Suarez who was on site observing tapped each support with a steel hammer and noted the difference in pitch. Based on this we adjusted the final post-tensioning forces. He practiced the *art* of engineering as well as its *science*!

The next day VSL verified that there were no significant losses of pre-stress force, and they gave the thumbs-up to install the remaining 50%. Out on the scaffold platform, we collectively held our breath as we watched the needle of the gauge on the hydraulic jack climb to its design level. A united sigh was heard—nothing out of the ordinary had occurred. We had done it successfully.

Finally, the strands were locked off and cut, and the holes in the south parapet patched.

Although the edges of the doubly cantilevered terraces had deflected more than 7 inches and the ends of the single cantilevered girder more than 5 inches, we never intended to try to raise the building back up to the level position. Over its sixty-year life, the plaster on the walls and ceilings, as well as the glass and the window and door frames, had all adjusted to or been modified to accept these movements. Had we tried to straighten it, all of the brittle finishes would have suffered severe damage and required drastic repairs. Thus the ends of the girder picked up off the temporary shoring only about ¾ inch, exactly as calculated. These movements were carefully charted throughout the post-tensioning process using both electronic and visual monitors.

Other small supplementary repairs were made throughout the structure.

At the conclusion of the structural work, a new subflooring system of purlins and plywood was put down, over which the stone floor was carefully reinstalled. The built-in wooden furniture was returned to the house, the temporary shoring removed, the exterior repainted, and when all was done, the house looked as it always had.

Of course it was left in a permanently deflected position, but this is part of its story. However, it is now safe for future generations to enjoy and visit with no further structural maintenance required for the main cantilevers.

WRIGHT IN THE WOODS: THE NATURE OF FALLINGWATER'S LANDSCAPE

By Rick Darke

Fallingwater is immersed in one of North America's most architectural landscapes. The mixed hardwoods that clothe this rocky western Pennsylvania region give sturdy form to forests built of intricate detail. This is a landscape of lines and layers, of luminous frames and infinite spaces. Intensely seasonal, it moves continually through familiar cycles while myriad elements and events are uniquely reprised and recast. The Kaufmanns knew this landscape as their own, and Wright knew it intuitively from lifelong experiences in similar Wisconsin woods. The spirit, insights, and ethics they brought to the making of Fallingwater so authentically conserved the vibrancy of the place that its nature is virtually undiminished seventy-five years later.

What is the essential nature of Fallingwater's landscape? The falls on Bear Run was the principal destination long before the house was imagined, yet iconic as it has become, the falls is only the most obvious element in a wondrous array of things and living processes that change at different paces. Wright recognized a fundamental "law of organic change" and believed all things to be in a continuous state of flux, no matter how subtle. He held this law to be so profoundly important that he stated it was the "only thing mankind can know as beneficent or as actual." Wright deeply valued the freedom and heightened awareness that can result from the celebration of change, and at Bear Run he made this the deliberate aim of his design.

Wright's autobiographical recollections say much about the enduring influence of observational experiences he enjoyed early in life exploring Wisconsin's woods and fields. Describing himself as insatiably curious and venturesome, he writes of learning to "know the woods, from the trees above to the shrubs below" and "the millions of curious lives hidden in the surface of the ground, among roots, stems, and mold." He delighted in learning the landscape through "experience, the only true reading." He tuned his senses at all hours, noting "sunlight, aslant through the leaves on the tree-trunks, plashing the leaf-covered ground beneath" as well as "night shadows, so wonderfully blue, like blue shadows on snow." Wright's practice of reading from natural phenomena closely followed the teachings of Ralph Waldo Emerson, who was much admired by Wright's nonconformist Welsh Unitarian family. Emerson was the principal proponent of American Transcendentalism's celebration of the incidental as key to the universal, and in *Nature* (1836), he wrote, "Not the sun nor the summer alone but every hour and season yields its tribute of delight: for every hour and change corresponds to and authorizes a different state of mind from breathless moon to grimmest midnight." By the time Wright met Kaufmann he had incorporated these observations and beliefs in a design ethic dedicated to revealing and accentuating the dynamic nature of the landscape.

Landscape design has traditionally been dedicated to control. The site is cleared and graded, waters are channeled or dammed, spaces are ordered, plants are installed in precise locations, and subsequent resources are devoted to maintaining the results in a static condition. Wright followed none of this at Bear Run. Traditional planting beds and borders are virtually absent. Instead, as he had done at his own Wisconsin home, Taliesin, Wright began with an inventory of the existing natural features and gently edited, preserving all possible. He fit his architecture deftly into the landscape, respecting the site's living character and ensuring that its dynamics would continue long after his work was completed. The woodland's lush growth was left wild and Bear Run's power continued unchecked.

page 272: Fallingwater is revealed gradually through windows in the woods flanking the approach. The arrangement of the openings—the forest's fenestration—changes with time of day and time of year. In this mid-April view the forest is still coming into leaf and is largely transparent. Delicate lateral branches repeat the horizontal planes of the house while the near-vertical lines of tree trunks provide strong visual counterpoints. A few more weeks of growth will close many of the windows from this perspective and visitors will be required to walk further for a first glimpse of Wright's architecture.

fig. 1

Imagining a walk in the western Pennsylvania woods is a superb way to understand the experiential nature of Fallingwater's architecture. From any distant clearing, the wooded landscape appears visually complex. Myriad crossing branches create literal windows—the forest's fenestration—that sometimes frame clear views to interior spaces and at other times provide only glimpses of deeper intrigues. Though evidently full of opportunity for exploration, rarely does the woods present an obvious point of entry. No matter where you choose to enter, the feathered edge of the forest makes it impossible to say precisely when you have left the clearing and are now inside the woods. A dense understory may initially envelope you, concentrating your awareness on the woodland's closer confines. Or you may duck under low branches to emerge in a greater space defined by tall trunks and a high canopy, and if so there is an elating sense of arrival. Rooms defined by trees and terrain appear in all sizes, offering intimacy or immensity. Shelter may be found under a ledge or under the cantilevered branches of a great oak, just as dizzying exposure may be sought at the edge of a high rocky ridge. In the absence of a marked trail, your journey will be guided by practicality and possibility, and your sense of purpose will influence your pace. The path forward will be guided by your desire to experience variations in the forest's furnishings. Textures and colors, sounds and scents, sunlight and shadow, vistas and obscurities will continually evolve as you move through space and time. As you step through an unprogrammed series of destinations, dramas bold and subtle may last for minutes or only for moments. Silhouettes of leafy tracery may appear etched on a smooth trunk or a rounded stone; turn your head to the call of a wood thrush, and in mere seconds the shadow patterns will be transformed or vanish entirely. If you begin in the morning and return near sundown, places you witnessed earlier may appear so altered they become refreshingly unfamiliar. Retrace your steps in another season or in another year and your awareness of the inexorable change in the forest's patterns and processes will be forever heightened, your visual acuity forever enhanced. With Fallingwater, Wright created architecture inseparable from the woods and similar in its capacity as an engine for seeing.

The layered form and luminous intricacy Wright built into Fallingwater ensure that the house is in sync with the forest with each step, with every passage, in every season. Wright's choreography of spaces evokes the woods as it emulates it. You can literally go for a walk within Fallingwater, moving from dark to light or from intimate rooms to the virtual infinity of the terraces. Like the woods, Fallingwater blends security and shelter with exploration and discovery. You may choose to linger in the heart of the house surrounded by stone or venture to the edge of the parapets, exploring the expanse above, below, and beyond to the very limits of comfort. Wright believed people derive "sustenance from the 'atmosphere' of the things they live in or with" and in the rejuvenative capacity of natural process. He believed in the necessity of architecture that would ensure people experience natural phenomena while going about life's routine journeys.

Is Fallingwater's landscape a wilderness? No. But is it wild? Certainly so. Trees growing around the house site prior to construction included birch, butternut, hickory, tulip poplar, maple, and various oaks, and virtually all of these species are still present; not just a few aging relicts but a multitude of individuals of all ages from seedling stage on up. Niches integral to the house provide functional habitats that sustain self-perpetuating populations, and these niches segue seamlessly with the varied habitats that make up the enveloping forest. It all looks easy and natural because it, in fact, is. The still-rich flora and fauna of Fallingwater's woods and waters owe their vibrancy to a stewardship model that recognizes the relationship between unfettered process and sustainable diversity.

Perhaps with the exception of Taliesin, Fallingwater's landscape context is the most enduringly authentic of all Wright sites. In contrast to the multitude of Wright landscapes that have been compromised or rendered unrecognizable by development, Fallingwater still sits amidst woodland whose essential character remains intact. These woods are now within the Western Pennsylvania Conservancy's Bear Run Nature Reserve, which comprises over five thousand acres and provides a protected forest buffer more extensive today than when the house was built. As in Edgar Kaufmann's era, the last miles approaching Fallingwater still take visitors through a patchwork of small towns, farms, and forests, eventually arriving in the richly wooded landscape of the house and falls.

This is not to suggest the place is unchanged. The region's cultural landscapes and ecologies have evolved in response to forces near and distant. Victims of an introduced fungal blight, the magnificent chestnut trees once prevalent in Allegheny forests were dead or dying by the time Fallingwater was begun, yet oaks and other hardwoods have increased naturally to fill the vacancies. The forest today again stands tall, but of recent concern is the regional arrival of the introduced woolly aphid, which has the potential to eliminate hemlocks from Bear Run.

Fallingwater was born of industry and enabled by technology, and each of these forces has impacted the regional landscape. The coal and steel industries that enriched the patrons of Kaufmann's department store once decimated forests and acidified waters, yet they also indirectly enabled the Kaufmann family to create Fallingwater and eventually to entrust it to the conservancy. It is fortunate that logging and mining activities at the periphery of the Fallingwater site ceased when they did. Although Edgar Kaufmann reforested some damaged areas with Norway spruces and other evergreens following forestry models of the period, these are now among the least diverse of Bear Run's forests. Many other areas were allowed to regenerate on their own, and the forests resulting from this approach are rich with indigenous flora and fauna. These woods owe their health to the fact that they regrew in an era prior to the overwhelming presence of highly competitive exotic species. The dynamics of forest regeneration have changed dramatically in the decades since Fallingwater was built. Introduced exotic plants are now among the first to colonize disturbed sites, in many cases altering successional patterns so profoundly that the character of resulting woods, wetlands, and meadows is radically altered. The conservancy's challenge and opportunity is to minimize future disturbance and to intervene wisely, observing carefully and developing management strategies appropriate for the varied niches in a diverse, continually evolving landscape.

The dynamics of Fallingwater and its living surrounds are indelibly linked. Wright knew the immersive experience of the combination would forever enliven the sensibilities of anyone who spends time in it. He set out to create a house disciplined by ideals, and he succeeded in crafting an environment that offers a scalable model for modern living. Never before or after in his long career did Wright have the opportunity to build in such an extraordinary landscape. And never before or after did Wright so confidently move beyond abstraction to articulate the actual.

Though Bear Run's slopes are clothed in vast stretches of evergreen rhododendron, the predominance of deciduous trees is the basis for the forest's supreme seasonality. The leaves' translucent qualities, especially as they emerge and again in late autumn, make this one of the most luminous landscapes on earth. Beeches stretch horizontally in this mid-May image capturing the peak of the new greens. These hues last a short while and then the foliage hardens and darkens for the remainder of the growing season. Wright knew and treasured such ephemeral beauty. In his autobiography he recalls learning "the look of it all in tender green or covered with snow or in full glow of summer that bursts into glorious blaze of autumn."

Shadows of rhododendron, also known
as great laurel, are a reliable part of the
integral ornament of boulders in and
along Bear Run's rocky course.

The immediacy of Fallingwater's
living landscape makes myriad seasonal
phenomena inescapable. Like Wright,
Emerson understood the unique impact
of encountering natural phenomena in
the course of everyday tasks, saying (in
his book *Nature*), "Go out of the house
to see the moon and 'tis mere tinsel; it
will not please as when its light shines on
your necessary journey." Wright went
beyond Emerson's words and crafted an
immersive architecture. Through the
deft use of transparency, framing, and the
choreography of space, Wright invited
the myriad dramas of regional nature
into the routines of daily life.

Though Fallingwater lacks traditional planting beds and borders, there is habitat everywhere around the house. Varied niches sustain authentic wildness and provide conditions for all sorts of plants to begin life. Mosses flourish on wet vertical surfaces despite the power of the falls, their placement and patterns evolving with each season and each year in response to the waters' varying flow. Wright reveled in experiencing the dynamic nature of the surrounding environment, and conceived of change itself as an integral part of the ornamentation of Fallingwater.

By October the spring woods' honeyed greens are only a memory, now replaced by autumn's translucent ambers. The horizontal signatures of beech branches endure through the shifting colors of the seasons.

The bright scarlet of a black gum is highlighted by gold-hued sweet birches growing below Paradise Overlook, a rocky promontory that is only a short walk from Fallingwater.

Looking out through the woods from a
slope above Bear Run. At first glance this
might appear to be a fall image, however
it is actually mid April. Though warm
amber, orange, and red hues are most
dramatic in autumn, they are also present
in the spring landscape.

When the autumn sun slants in sharply
through the forest, Fallingwater's
surfaces become virtual movie screens,
displaying flickering silhouettes
of woodland patterns.

Like the landscape surrounding it,
Fallingwater is finished in varied textures
that respond visually to changing weather
and seasons. Wright believed houses
should have "such texture as will quiet the
whole and make it graciously at one with
external nature."

A wet January snow outlines a Laurel Highlands forest and illustrates the balance of trees and shrubs that have fitted to one another through years of incremental growth. Forever taking cues from actual landscapes, Wright described a new ideal of organic building "as dignified as a tree in the midst of nature." In scenes like this he recognized the quality of repose, which he considered the highest in the art of architecture. For Wright, repose meant that which is "perfectly adjusted in relation to the whole."

Boulders below the falls in deep January
snow, viewed from the warm comfort
of Fallingwater's interior.

APPENDIX: KAUFMANN ESSAYS

In 1940, The Museum of Modern Art mounted a major exhibition on the work of Frank Lloyd Wright in its newly completed home at 11 West 53rd Street in New York. The retrospective *Frank Lloyd Wright: American Architect* was to be accompanied by a catalogue that included essays by prominent historians, architects, and Wright clients (Peter Reed and William Kaizen, eds. *The Show to End All Shows: Frank Lloyd Wright and The Museum of Modern Art, 1940*, Studies in Modern Art, no.8 [New York: The Museum of Modern Art, 2004]). Working closely with Wright on both the design of the show and the catalogue, the endeavor was fraught with problems. It was not the exhibition's curator, John McAndrew's, first experience working with Wright. Two years earlier he had curated the exhibition that introduced Fallingwater to the world: *A New House by Frank Lloyd Wright on Bear Run, Pennsylvania,* which showed at the museum's temporary quarters in the underground concourse of the Time Life Building at 14 West 49th Street. While the Fallingwater show was put together with little advance planning when a slot opened in the exhibition schedule (because of the postponement of a major Alvar Aalto show), this more comprehensive Frank Lloyd Wright exhibition was the result of several years of planning.

Nevertheless, with only two months to go before the opening, McAndrew decided to abandon the catalogue out of frustration with Wright's demands for editorial control. The following essays by Edgar Kaufmann Sr., Liliane Kaufmann, and Edgar Kaufmann jr. were commissioned for the catalogue to provide the client's perspective.

In his essay, "To Meet—To Know—To Battle—To Love—Frank Lloyd Wright," Edgar Kaufmann Sr. recounts the birth of Fallingwater from his first meeting with Wright (whom he always refers to as "The Master") through to the building's completion. From his carefully reconstructed recollections, we see a charmingly witty and savvy businessman very much Wright's equal, who to achieve his objective approaches the process with planning and discipline in much the same way he would approach any business transaction. One interesting feature of his chronological account is that nowhere does he mention the famous visit to Taliesin described by Edgar Tafel in his memoir *Years with Frank Lloyd Wright: Apprentice to Genius* and corroborated by two other apprentices who were there, Wes Peters and Bob Mosher, in Kenneth Love's film, *The Apprentices.* All three recalled in vivid detail how Wright, surrounded by amazed apprentices who could not sharpen his pencils quickly enough, "shook the design out of his sleeve" in the few hours it took Kaufmann, anxious to see the long awaited design for his weekend house, to drive from Milwaukee to Spring Green. Years ago I asked Edgar Tafel about this omission. He concluded that although he and the others present understood Wright's rough sketches created that busy morning, it was entirely likely that Kaufmann did not. It was only after the plans arrived in Pittsburgh and Kaufmann had the time to study them that he gained a true understanding of the design.

Liliane Kaufmann offers us the point of view of the mistress of the house, providing a very personal account of what it was like to live in Fallingwater. For her it required adjustments. She lists the challenges of limited closet space and not enough room for the proper storage of the linens, china, and other things necessary to the running of a great house. But with grace and humility she also expresses her gratitude to Wright for opening her eyes to the beauty of materials plainly expressed and educating her to the value of living more simply.

page 300: Portrait of the Kaufmann family at Fallingwater, circa 1940, taken by Luke Swank and displayed in a gilt bronze frame with inlaid abalone by Tiffany Studios.

Edgar Kaufmann jr. focuses his essay on the interiors. In 1940 he was named a curator and later director of MoMA's Department of Industrial Design where he initiated the Good Design program of 1950–55, in which the museum joined forces with the Merchandise Mart in Chicago to promote good design in household objects and furnishings. In the essay he describes the family's program for Fallingwater as "easy living" appropriate to a weekend house and recounts the give and take between Wright and the family as together they worked to achieve that goal. The result is a thoughtful analysis of the role the interiors play in creating the organic whole that is Fallingwater.

"To meet—to know—to battle—to love—Frank Lloyd Wright"
By Edgar J. Kaufmann Sr.

1934

In the fall of 1934 Mrs. Kaufmann and I traveled to Taliesin to visit our son, who was there as a member of the Taliesin Fellowship. We were met by the charming and beautiful Mrs. Wright, her daughters, Iovanna and Svetlana, and the police dog.

During the afternoon we became gradually acquainted with some of the fellows, and had a visit with the Master and his family before an informal dinner with him and the children. I remember distinctly the homemade wine. Mr. and Mrs. [George S.] Parker (of the pens) joined the weekend.

After dinner, conversation in small groups. Then sudden silence. Music. Edgar Tafel, one of the fellows, playing Bach-then-Beethoven. Silence again. A semicircle was formed and the Master spoke.

He discussed with the fellows the reconditions and rehabilitation of the model of Broadacre City [project 1934–34]. The Master called upon Mr. Parker. The fellows listened attentively. I realized I was in for something. What should I say? The Master gave the cue and I expressed my interest in the rehabilitation of the Broadacre model. I wanted to know more about it, and the fellows promised to show me the model and explain it the following day. It was whispered that money was needed. I listened but was not particularly interested.

Edgar Kaufmann Sr. in his department store office, circa 1940. *Western Pennsylvania Conservancy.*

The fellows retired. The house was quiet. Around a smoldering fire, one of the many delightful ones in the house of the Taliesin, sat the Master, Mr. Parker, and myself. The conversation was general. Finally the master challenged me: "What are your interests besides selling rags?" At that particular time, I told him, I was deeply interested in the Allegheny County Authority, which had come into existence partly through my efforts and which was contemplating building a number of bridges and a viaduct around the riverfronts of Pittsburgh's Golden Triangle; I had been negotiating for a planetarium in Pittsburgh. Furthermore, I hoped to find a scheme to reconditioning my own office. The one I was using I had lived with for ten years. And, not least, we had been dreaming of a lodge to take care of the family all year round from innumerable mountain springs and finally emptying into the Youghigheny River. The Master was interested. He wanted to talk more about it the next day.

Sunday morning, immediately after breakfast, cars and trucks were loaded with lunch baskets and equipment for a morning in the Wisconsin woods. It was a beautiful day, with clear-cut skylines and big trees. Extreme informality prevailed. On the way one gets better acquainted with the fellows and the Master. Then a hurried trip back to Taliesin for Sunday afternoon moving pictures. Visitors from everywhere. Finally a late inspection and explanation of the Broadacre model. It intrigued me and I committed myself to help to rehabilitate it. In the morning the Master promised to send it to Pittsburgh for exhibition to the citizens of the Tri-State area.

After dinner and more music from records and from Edgar Tafel, we had to depart. A promise was exacted that I should visit the workshop at Chandler, Arizona, during the coming winter, where the Broadacre model was to be worked on. In return a promise from the Master to come to Pittsburgh within the next fortnight to meet the Allegheny County Authority Commission. There

pages 304–315: Text of Kaufmann essays appearing on these pages are reproduced from Registrar Exhibition Files, Exh. #114. *The Museum of Modern Art Archives, New York.*

might be hope of making some arrangement for him to become consulting engineer and architect. The two-day meeting in December 1934 ended without success. They simply did not understand. The Master looked at my office and made suggestions for the new one. I did not understand but he promised to put it on paper. We discussed a planetarium and he made rough sketches. But we left that for the moment because we were hurrying to Bear Run to look over the possible site of the lodge, later to known as Fallingwater.

The sun was shining when we started. Unusual for Pittsburgh in December. We traveled through Clairton Valley along the Monongahela River admiring the powerful steelworks along its banks. A slight rain began to fall. On to Connellsville, where it turned into a light snow. Up over Chestnut Ridge—still snowing—then down toward Bear Run. Light rain with a magnificent rainbow which crossed the mountains and dipped into both valleys greeted us as we arrived. The Master in a comfortable seat had been relaxing. With the rainbow he became alive. Turning to me he said, "Surely something will come out of this journey; after all the elements through which we have traveled, the end is crowned with a rainbow."

We tramped around the terrain of waterfalls. The Master was amazed at the beauty and forceful contours. His first idea was a house suspended by cable from cliff to cliff, facing the falls. I stood amazed. We talked and disagreed. It ended by my promising to send a topographical map which was to include everything 100 feet above and 200 feet below the falls, showing every tree more than 2" in diameter, and every stone and boulder permitted, by the ages, to rear its head above the ground.

1935

In February we spent two weeks in Arizona, eighteen hours a day with the Master and fellows. It was the busiest workshop I have ever lived with. Planning, thinking, discussing—Broadacre City was gradually being rehabilitated with fury. Larger models explaining certain features were being constructed. It was a fascinating fortnight.

Further discussions of the office, the planetarium, and the Allegheny County Authority projects. The Master asked how we wanted to live in our Bear Run house. I explained we had been living in a 40" x 40" Aladdin House with screen sleeping porches on three sides. On the fourth side had been constructed a living room 40"x60", with solid logs for three feet, and above that removable windows. A little pool, fed by mountain spring water, ten steps away from my bed. We had been living and sleeping practically in the open, bathing in cold water before breakfast, all day, and after dinner. Simplified housekeeping, a minimum of servants and house cares.

We discussed material. There was plenty of native stone handy to the site; plenty of river sand within less than half a mile; plenty of white and black oak, poplar and fir, and a saw mill within 1/8 of a mile. I asked what he had in mind. Where would the house be placed? What would it look like? The Master was silent. How many rooms do you want? We need a utility room, a kitchen, a living room large enough for eating, living and music, and double guestroom and bath, a double master's bedroom and bath, a single master's dressing room and bath for overflow guests, a single bedroom and bath for Junior. I stress our habit of living outdoors, behind screen or behind glass.

We had learned to allow the outside to come in. More discussion. What would it look like? Where would we place it? Again the Master was silent. Wait until the contour plan comes.

On Mar 9 the topographical survey was sent to Mr. Wright. During April the fellows were working on a project.

On April 27 a letter arrived: "We are ready to go to work on the waterfall cottage at Bear Run and the planetarium. Also we are like the little Mississippi River steamboat Lincoln told about—every time she blew her whistle she had to heave to at the bank for steam. We blew our whistle so long and loud on Broadacre that we have nothing left." Fifteen hundred dollars needed, forty oriental prints as security—the loan to be paid off in eighteen months, the prints to be returned. Instead, I sent the $1,500.00 as an advance on the house.

May: Broadacre completed. Caravan from Arizona to New York.

June 15: Broadacre came to Pittsburgh for a two-week exhibit. Howling success. Miners, mill workers, white-collar workers deeply interested; few architects during the first week; few of the upper crust. Second week—more architects, plenty of upper crust. Exhibit closed in a blaze of glory.

September 15: Floor plans and colored elevation of Fallingwater arrived. The next few nights were sleepless. Finally I began to understand the plan partially. The Master's conception—the colored elevations fascinated me. At least I thought I understood.

On September 16 I could not work. I thought of nothing but the house.

September 21: The Master arrived. Went over the plan thoroughly. Allowed me to drink in his conception and the meaning. My first lesson in organic architecture/it was plain and I did not understand—it required the Master to open my eyes.

He also discussed his idea of an all-wood office. Again, I did not understand at all. He talked about a plywood mural at one end. I was more confused than ever. My mind was on Fallingwater. The office had to be pushed aside.

The following Sunday a new vision of the house grew upon me and I stood on the rocks with Junior and Mrs. Kaufmann-we read the plan and discussed it.

The Master came to Pittsburgh to speak at the Hungry club in October; he demanded the destruction of all Pittsburgh and its rebuilding. He caused consternation to the reading public of the evening and morning papers and provoked many editorial comments pro and anti.

In December we decided to quarry stone during the winter for a possible beginning of Fallingwater the following spring. The walls to be minimum 18" thick; stones to be the run of the quarry. Those split thinner than 4" to be kept aside as paving stones throughout the house and terraces.

Edgar Kaufmann jr., Frank Lloyd Wright, and Edgar Kaufmann Sr. at Taliesin West, 1947. © *Pedro E. Guerrero.*

1936

Late February finally a letter from Chandler with a package, "We have sent you in this morning's mail two complete sets of blueprints of Fallingwater. Three copies of specifications."

In May the quarrying had been completed. A sample wall had been constructed at the quarry.

The Master arrived on his way to Philadelphia to inspect the sample wall for an hour. Not satisfied, he made correction. "I don't have much confidence in any of the usual estimates you can get on this work. We will have to plan some way of taking it up more directly with some interested competent builder who is small enough to stay on the job and experienced enough to know what to do and how to do it with out help." I query, "Where do you find such?" The Master answers, "I had one but he is too old. He has built many of my buildings. We will have to find a new one."

This was very discouraging because I realized that the proper man was needed to interpret, and to understand how to build according to the Master's interpretation.

The latter part of April, we turned over plans and specifications to our estimating, purchasing, and building department. They, in turn, wrote a four-page letter to the Master asking for further explanation. The Master returned the original letter to me with priceless marginal notes.

Early in May a letter came from Taliesin:

> *You seem to forget all I said about building an extraordinary house in extraordinary circumstances. Having been through it scores of times I know what we are up against and decline to start it unless I can see our way. The same to you. Now suppose I were a sculptor and you would say "Carve me an extraordinary statue." I would accept. Then you hand me a pantograph and say—"Use this. I have found the use of the pantograph is a good way to carve statues. It saves time and money." Then I would say—"But in this case it will waste time and money and ruin the statue." You would come back with "But when I have statues made I have the pantograph used."*
>
> *Well E. J., you would have the sculptor where you have me now with your Thumm.3 I can't build this extraordinary house with a Thumm. Read the enclosed correspondence and note the pantograph punctilio for only one thing. There is no sense whatever of the things he should know after studying the plans.*
>
> *Now a pickaxe is more suited to my style of labor than a pantograph. But, for a fact, I can't use either.*
>
> *Your Thumm won't do. I must have my own fingers. . . .*
>
> *This ought to clear up point one and get me a modest builder with brains—not too anxious to show off—willing to learn new ways of doing old things: able but wise to the fact that his previous experience might fool him in this case. . . .*

Finally first check sent on account for bridge detail and specifications. Taliesin wires two days later—"Check has been mislaid, please send duplicate."

May 15: Ten strikes. The Master writes that his son from California has been motorcycling through Pennsylvania near Port Allegany, McKean County, when he stopped his car abruptly because he recognized the earmarks of the Master's design on what was called a Tea House and Filling Station. He inquired of the two maiden ladies who built the building. It had been a local contractor by the name of Walker J. Hall & Son. The son immediately wired the Master, "Here is a possible builder for the Kaufmann project." The Master corresponded with Hall and Hall said he was interested.

On May 27th I telephoned Hall asking him to come to Pittsburgh and he was most eager to build a building designed by Frank Lloyd Wright.

I tried to get him to give us a bid at once. By June 14 his estimates were received. In the meantime I looked up his references and personal credit rating. He had always been known as the efficient carpenter and builder, and had done some contracting on his own account, but during the last eight years had little to do. His reputation was good; he was well liked by the workmen.

I communicated with the Master. He was happy with the results. This was exactly the kind of man he wanted. Mr. Hall became superintendent in charge of construction.

He accepted and by July 13 he started work and the building was begun. He organized local farmers and their boys to do carpentry, smithing, masonry, and concrete work. (Plumbing, electrical work, and heating were of course installed by trained workmen.)

There was some question about the safety of the site for the type of building the Master submitted, so I commissioned an engineer's report. It arrived on July 18 and did not recommend the site for an important structure, for the rate of recession of the falls, although slow, could not be predicted with any degree of safety. There was evidence of minor spalling off of the rock at the face of the falls and a possibility of further disturbance of the rock strata if channels were cut in the surface to provide necessary keyways for the foundation walls.

> The questions of utilizing the boulder as a base of the fireplace is perhaps a detail, but we do not consider the boulder suitable for incorporation into the foundation of the building.
>
> Of course there is a possibility, or even a probability, that future deterioration of the rock ledge will not be sufficient to endanger the foundations; but in our opinion there could be no feeling of complete safety and consequently we recommend that the proposed site be not used for any important structure.

I was in a quandary. I did not communicate with the Master. I figured periodic inspections could be made regarding recession and if any alarming condition did arise it could be caught and rectified. I knew it was difficult to say just what nature might do, but in most cases there was always evidence showing before any real danger. No record as to when the minor spalling referred to by the engineer had occurred—but they were due to frost action in the upper stratifications as verified by the profile of the falls. The engineer misinterpreted Wright's plan, for it had not been intended to use keyways in the foundation work. Moreover, I was not prepared to sacrifice using the boulder for the fireplace under any circumstances.

We did not stop work. We filed the engineer's report.

On July 27, Bob Mosher, one of the fellows at Taliesin, arrived to interpret the plans and assist Mr. Hall. From now on the work became exciting. I spent most of my days helping in the interpretation of the plans and in the construction.

On August 2, the steel diagrams arrived. They were sent out for estimates.

Steel engineers questioned the specifications of reinforcing as well as the general steel and concrete construction. Hall, Mosher, and myself got into a huddle one afternoon and decided to proceed with the Master's specifications. To cap the climax the engineers who had condemned the site appeared, were surprised that we had started work, and began to tell their story to Hall and Mosher.

Edgar Kaufmann Sr. fishing at McGregor Bay, Ontario, 1930s. *Western Pennsylvania Conservancy.*

Word reached Taliesin. Out of the blue on Sunday morning came the following telegram to Mosher: "The battle of Bear Run is on. Drop work and come back immediately. We are through until Kaufmann and I arrive at some basis of mutual respect. You are needed here. Do not delay one hour and bring in all the plans you can get . . . Frank Lloyd Wright."

We were crestfallen. The day became bluer. We suggested that Bob telephone. The result—another telegram: "You are at least able to get off job as expected. Neither explanation nor argument should be necessary. Affairs there are more serious than you comprehend. If you are unable or unwilling to carry out my instructions your connection with me ends. I am not coming to Pittsburgh. More sleepless nights.

August 27: The following letter from Taliesin:

> *If you are praying to have the concrete engineering done there, there is no use whatever in our doing it here. I am willing you should take it over but I am not willing to be insulted.*
>
> *So we will send no more steel diagrams. I am unaccustomed to such treatment where I have built buildings before and do not intend to put up with it now so I am calling Bob back until we can work out something or nothing . . .*

August 28: How should I answer? I did the best I could:

> *If you have been paid to do the concrete engineering up there, there is no use whatever of our doing it down here. I am not willing to take it over as you suggest nor am I willing to be insulted.*
>
> *So if you will not send any more steel diagrams, what shall I do? I am unaccustomed to such treatment where I have been building before and I do not intend to put up with it now so I am calling you to come down here, which I hoped you could have done during the past few weeks, to inspect the work under Mr. Hall's direction who is an unknown foreman to you, instead of allowing the entire responsibility of his craftsmanship to rest upon us here. So if you will come here perhaps we can work out something or nothing . . .*
>
> *PS: Now don't you think that we should stop writing letters and that you owe it to the situation to come to Pittsburgh and clear it up by getting the facts? Certainly there are reasons which must have prompted you to write as you have.*
>
> *I am sorry that you are calling Bob back. He seems entirely wrapped up in his work and in its progress but this is beyond my control and you must use your own judgment . . .*

August 29: Bob, finally, with the help of the family, packed his two shirts, his one pair of work pants, two sweaters—we could not find his socks and his work shoes—and reluctantly put on his first Pittsburgh outfit for traveling back home. We all stood at the gate and waved him goodbye. It was not an easy moment.

August 31: Another letter from Taliesin only partly quoted:

> *Apologies are nothing to a man like yourself. But explanation seems to be in order. The atmosphere*

should be cleared. Lightning and inevitable thunder may help to clear it. Anyhow that's what it is as I see the way it is. The thing that hurts me in this instance I assure you. I am sure it hurts you.

Meantime your letter shows me that I do owe it to you and to myself to get on that job. I'll come soon. Sincerely, Frank Lloyd Wright.

The armistice is on. The Master leaves for Pittsburgh in early September. The parties to the armistice: Mr. Wright; Edgar Tafel, a fellow of Taliesin; Mr. Hall; and myself. It is not held in a railroad coach but under a majestic oak tree. The conditions are discussed and agreed to. Mr. Hall remains superintendent, Edgar Tafel is to take Bob Mosher's place on the first of October. Mr. Hall is to be sent to Taliesin in the early winter to absorb the spirit in which the drawings are turned out. I agreed not to inject myself or any of my "yes" men, as the Master called them, except through Edgar Tafel.

Much progress was made during Edgar's direction. Unfortunately he was called back to Taliesin November 22. The master was confined with a slight cold. In December word reached us that he was bedridden with pneumonia.

In a letter of November 2, the Master wrote:

> *I think you fail to realize how well off you have been in the execution of this building so far. Hall is rough but pretty good and all the mistakes made including the crooked bridge rails don't add up enough to form a fair basis for complaint.*
>
> *Perhaps you don't quite realize the nature of what is being done for you and still imagine it could have been done without error or waste by way of the present system. No more possible than for Franklin D. Roosevelt to give us a better government by way of "politics." Hall is doing remarkably well with awkward material.*

Edgar Kaufmann Sr. in his department store office, circa 1940. *Western Pennsylvania Conservancy.*

During the last week of Edgar's stay checks in the concrete work appeared on the terrace of the master bedroom. Edgar was concerned.

Before leaving we discussed with Edgar an arrangement to have engineers make computations of the structure every three months to see what was happening. In spite of the Master's illness the following telegram December 29:

> *KINDLY REFRAIN ALL INTERFERENCE WITH ME IN MY WORK AT THIS TIME, SEND ME WHAT I ASK FOR. HAVE NO RESPONSIBLE RERPESENTATIVE. IN THESE CIRCUMSTANCES EASY TO SPOIL THE ENTIRE WORK BY LACK OF CONFIDENCE IN MY ABILITY TO HANDLE MY OWN WORK. KINDLY STAND BY. CUT AND SEND ME THE CONCRETE SAMPLES AS DIRECTED. THEY WILL NOT HARM THE STRUCTURE. I WILL PAY FOR THEM IF IN THE OUTCOME IT SEEMS NECESSARY. I WANT AN UNCRACKED STRUCTURE. KNOW HOW TO GET IT. INTEND TO HAVE IT. READ MY LETTER MAILED YESTERDAY. IN CIRCUMSTANCES LIKE THESE THERE IS ONLY ONE DOCTOR. BE*

1937

The engineers, late December 1936, made complete investigation of the engineering features of Fallingwater, together with several loading tests of the structure itself. They made similar computations again on January 6, 1937, January 13, and May 21. Deflections at various points of the building showed only from 3/16" to ¾" maximum. The report: "The structure doers not have a satisfactory factor of safety, or what might be termed reserve strength."

On January 2, we sent samples of concrete to the Master, as he asked. He had them analyzed and they proved satisfactory.

The house was completed during the spring of 1937.

That summer Mr. and Mrs. Wright were invited to Russia for an International Conference of Architects.

On September 7, we had been wiring back and forth because the Master had not been to see the completed work.

On December 19 he finally came and spent the day inspecting and re-arranging many things. Nevertheless it was a day of rejoicing for both of us.

We discussed the extension. The Master surveyed the hillside on which it was to be built. He gave me a sketchy outline of what was in his mind.

1938

The winter closed us in at Bear Run. Hall was living like a squirrel in his little house on the terrace.

February 22: From Taliesin-in-the-Desert, Scottsdale, Arizona, comes the following letter: "When do you want to build the extension? We will try to have the plans then."

Letter relayed to Sun Valley, Idaho, where I was trying to learn to ski I answered the Master, "Intend to build at once."

April 26: Letter from Taliesin, Wisconsin: "Plans are in work."

May 25: Plans arrived with elevations. I wrote the Master that we were very enthusiastic about them but we find the addition too large.

On July 27 the Master came. We discussed revision of the guest wing, servants' quarters, and garage.

On August 20 a letter reading "All going well. Revision to guesthouse complete."

1938

On January 6, I informed the Master that Mr. Hall had agreed to start to build the guest wing, servant's quarters, and garage at once. This was the beginning of our second building operation. I spent most of January and the first two weeks in February on the site. I had been having trouble with my back, probably from falling off horses during the past thirty years, aggravated by having fallen not less than thirty times a day learning to ski.

The scene changes in March, to a hospital in New York. I am to undergo an operation—the first of my life. The Master has been called to England for a series of lectures—sailing April 25. Mrs. Kaufmann and the nurses say that coming out of the anesthesia that very morning, I shouted, "Send for Frank Lloyd Wright—send for Frank Lloyd Wright–there is something structurally wrong with me." That evening, when Mrs. Kaufmann bade Mr. and Mrs. Wright goodbye, she mentioned it to them.

From the R.M.S. *Queen Mary* I received the following letter, dated April 25, 1939:

> *I meant to get around to see you in New York before embarking on this errand to England but, as usual, got late and had to run.*
>
> *I was shocked to hear of so serious an operation but glad to know that you had it over with and now heading in for an end to physical torture. You must have suffered! The house addition was going swell when I saw it. Stonework beautiful. Hall doing well as could be, etc, etc.*
>
> *Junior is running things all right.*
>
> *Mrs. Kaufmann told me your remark when coming out from under ether—so apparently I have made a deep impression. Anyhow here's to you man. I hope this finds you cheerful and coming along to everybody's satisfaction—yours most of all. I expect great things of you—and Pittsburgh—I'll not forget the hand you gave me in my work and besides I like you a lot. To you, Liliane, and Junior, faithfully. Frank Lloyd Wright.*

On August 24 we made an inspection of the house. It was a great day. Perhaps more for myself than for anyone. That night we celebrated into the wee hours of the morning. I was going through my post-graduate course with the Master. Daylight was breaking for me. When he spoke, I understood, where two years before there had been blank. He has been a great inspiration and tolerant of my ignorance. I know that I am a better man for having met him, built with him, battled with him, and learned to love him.

September 12, 1939, comes the final telegram: "*DEAR E. J. IT'S PRETTY DRY HERE WE ARE WAITING AND HOPING FOR A LIFE WILL YOU? SIGNED FRANK.*"

September 14 I answer: "*GET OVER YOUR PARCHED FEELING WATER ON THE WAY. REGARDS, EDGAR*"

November 15—the last letter in my file from the Master: "*Dear Edgar—you were right in your surmise and I can't tell you how I appreciate your help where I guess I'll always need it most. Affection always Frank.*"

Untitled

By Liliane Kaufmann

For the past three years I have been learning to live in a Frank Lloyd Wright house. It has been an eye-opening experience and a constructive lesson in deletion.

I moved into the house with numerous misgivings, spoken and unspoken. I appreciated the architectural beauty of the exterior, but the interior seemed to me cold, barren, and monotonous. The closet space seemed inadequate and the housekeeping arrangements rudimentary, even for weekend living.

In a very short time, I decided that since I could not adapt the house to my way of living, I must adapt my way of living to the house. It proved to be surprisingly easy, and once the decision was made, my education had begun. It can be epitomized by using my own room as an example. When my eye had become accustomed to the lack of color and ornament, these two factors became apparent everywhere: I found ample color in the warm stones of my fireplace—in the stone floor and walls; the remaining plaster walls became a quiet background for two pictures at which I love to look. Lack of ornament brought out the amazing strength and loveliness of architectural line and detail. I began to glory in the sense of space and peace with which my room filled me. Leaf-laden trees or bare interlacing branches were a more-than-satisfactory substitute for curtains and draperies; a light-weight screen, easily rolled or unrolled, gave me the necessary privacy when I dressed; a sleep shade allowed me to sleep as late as I chose in spite of wide-open, unshaded windows. At the end of three years, I resent the smallest addition to the beautiful simplicity of my room.

Liliane Kaufmann at McGregor Bay, Ontario, 1930s. *Western Pennsylvania Conservancy.*

The matter of closet space was a revelation to me—I had grown up in a household where pile on top of pile of linens, blankets, and personal clothing was a sign and symbol of good housekeeping. I have learned that the reverse is true, and I house my perfectly adequate supply of linens with the greatest ease and order. Of course, I haven't any "good" linens—no separate guest sheets and pillowcases, no guest towels. I hope never to have any again. For the first few weeks my country clothes, sweaters and coats, filled two units of hanging space and two units of sliding shelves. By a delightful process of elimination, which involved keeping only the ones I liked and really wore, I find one entire unit of shelf-space as bare as Mother Hubbard's cupboard, and one unit of hanging space only sparsely filled. I began to understand what [Rudyard Kipling's] Kim meant when he said that "a Sahib is tied by his luggage." Perhaps Frank Lloyd Wright has taught me new appreciations of literature as well as of color and proportion.

Lest anyone reading this should think that I have achieved supreme satisfaction in the matter of living and keeping house at Fallingwater, I must also list the grievances that I still harbor: I find the kitchen too small when we have crowded weekends; I have not enough space to keep china and glassware in the orderly fashion which they deserve; and I should have liked a small separate storage room for extra chairs for the dining table, extra occasional tables, additional breakfast trays for guests, etc.

Perhaps these are the vestigial remains of my previously undeveloped standards—they may disappear with the rest in another year when I have learned to live the Wright way.

REG, EXH. #114. *MoMA Archives.*

Untitled

By Edgar Kaufmann jr.

The interiors of our house are planned for easy living, and in the hope that the same spirit that formed the architecture would be projected into a new field with different materials, functions, and a different scale. Naturally, we depended on Mr. Wright for designs and suggestions. He had built a background of stone piers—light gray with considerable variation into warmer tints of ocher and iron oxide red. He used the same stone for floors, with a beautiful rippled surface, just as it came from the quarry up the hill, but lightly varnished and waxed, giving a greater range of light and dark. The concrete surfaces and occasional plaster walls are finished in waterproof concrete paint, colored very light rosy ocher. Since the shapes flow in and out past the glass weather-shield, the color was held inside and out alike. The frames for glass are painted a dark iron red, called Cherokee. The window areas are left bare everywhere except for Venetian blinds in the two guest bedrooms. Against generous sweeps of these vivid yet austere materials in the winding recesses of Mr. Wright's airy caverns, we planned the furnishing of our house.

A big portion of the main furniture Mr. Wright built in-and he held certain simple features constant throughout. The shapes are large and rectangular. The wood is black walnut with sap streaks, unstained—its color value not unlike the window frames. Upholstery is latex rubber foam of varying resiliencies (which we still find very comfortable after three years of use). Echoing the cantilever of the main structure, the main blocks of the furniture (including cupboards) have been kept six inches above the floor; the supports rarely show. An expanse of one material often stops several inches short of its neighboring material. This can be seen in the first photograph where the bench back avoids the stone pier; only the top, horizontal wood surface and the seat continue through to join them. At the radiator box to the right of the dinning area this was not possible, and the wood panel overlaps the stone instead. With these and a few more simple details, Mr. Wright gave the principal built-in elements a calm unity, and a feeling of kinship with the stone-and-concrete structure.

When we were ready to move in, some features of the big room, as Mr. Wright planned it, were lacking. His furniture layouts had always shown large carpets, even on the stairs. Five reflector floor lamps in the main room were supposed to supplement the ceiling lights of the central and dining areas. We did not yet have any movable chairs with backs or arms.

By the end of the first winter we were sure that large floor coverings would be only stuffy. This perhaps because the heating worked so well, and we had no drafts.

Natural monks' cloth covered the slats of main benches and the higher stools, and some of the square but soft back-cushions—after all, why need to scold five lively long-haired dogs every time they come in from running in the woods? Our splurge of color came in the majority of back-cushions and the double-faced ottomans on the floor—there we used the brightest red, yellow, and green we could find. Later, after trying blue, we confined ourselves to red and soft yellow and to a few down pillows in bright patterned fabrics that struck our fancy.

Edgar Kaufmann jr., 1932. *Western Pennsylvania Conservancy.*

Note to reader: this essay originally held references to illustrations as well as image captions. Image references and captions are not included here. For this material, please refer to original document in the archives of the Museum of Modern Art. REG, EXH. #114. *MoMA Archives.*

The coffee table first had higher, stiffer cushions with small square tops. These we never grew to like and replaced them by the upturned stumps you see. (The chestnuts on our ridge were blighted as everywhere in the east twenty years ago, and we had been using their wood as firewood, and fences, and the stumps as tables, ever since we first came to Bear Run, fourteen years before.) To the coffee tables were added two copper-topped tables for drinks, one near the hearth for winter (and near the kettle Mr. Wright gave us to heat wine over the fire), one near the terrace doors for summer.

At the dining table we use peasant chairs from Tuscany, three legged, with uncarved but flamboyantly silhouetted backs. Although Mr. Wright recommended the metal chairs with circular backs and seats used in the [S. C.] Johnson [& Son, Inc.] Administration Building [Racine, Wisconsin, 1937–39], we have never been willing to replace the old ones. Through the room itself, and elsewhere, Mr. Wright suggested first the light barrel chair, made of slats, that he revised from earlier efforts for the Johnson residence ["Wingspread," the Herbert F. Johnson House, Racine, 1937–39], to be made in black walnut for our house. Later he showed us drawings of another armchair. Both seemed more formal than we wished, and the first, on sample, not loungy enough. So we started with canvas camp chairs and ended with the webbed chairs by Bruno Mathsson. [T]he same chair, with reading arm and pillow, is disguised by a mountain-goat-skin over the chair and a red-and-white Indian rug over the pillow. Elsewhere we have used modern chairs of Swedish or German design, or some by our friend and frequent guest [Laszlo] Gabor,[1] who also designed our outdoor chairs in webbing. We have quite a few [Alvar] Aalto chairs too, but they seem happiest in the only rooms with curtains.

Samples of two different floor lamps were made and proved unsatisfactory. We turned to the lighting experts, and never were experts more stumped; their usual solutions were defeated everywhere, and new ones not forthcoming. Eventually, with Mr. Wright's consent, we put fluorescent strips in the radiator ledges behind the benches. They work excellently, giving strong light for reading, and even light up the outdoor shrubbery and eaves enough to maintain some of the daytime continuity of outdoors with indoors.

Thus, gradually, after trial and error, our big problems have evaporated, leaving us a house we love to live in, flexible, still growing. We wanted a medium for relaxation; for this the architecture is ideal, and the furnishings, we feel, follow and heighten it to the degree we have been able to absorb and understand Mr. Wright's organic conception.

Kaufmann Family Letters: Edgar Kaufmann jr., Frank Lloyd Wright, and Fallingwater **by David G. De Long**

1. Letter, Liliane to Edgar jr., undated [F227]. Numbers in brackets refer to uncatalogued correspondence; they designate the folder (as "F") and the sequential position of the letter within that folder. Numbers in parenthesis record the number of catalogued correspondence.
2. Letters, Edgar Sr. to Edgar jr., December 29, 1927 (C055 and C094), and January 20, 1928 (C058). Edgar jr.'s address, Apt. 5-G, 685 Lexington Avenue, New York City, is cited in a letter from Edgar Sr. to Edgar jr., January 12, 1928 (C057).
3. Letter, Purdy to Edgar jr., October 12, 1927 (G003); also undated (G100); and April 8, 1928 (G42). For discussion of Edgar jr.'s early studies, Franklin Toker, *Fallingwater Rising: Frank Lloyd Wright, E. J. Kaufmann, and America's Most Extraordinary House* (New York: Alfred A. Knopf, 2003), especially 359–62. Papers related to the Ferargil Galleries are in the Archives of American Art, the Smithsonian.
4. Letter, Purdy to Edgar jr., July 2, 1929 (G022).
5. Letter, Liliane to Edgar jr., undated [F227].
6. Letter, Edgar jr. to Purdy, undated [G162].
7. Letter, Edgar jr. to Purdy, March 14 [1929] (C020).
8. Letter, Edgar jr. to Purdy, March 23 [1929] (G029).
9. Letter, Edgar jr. to Edgar Sr., September 23, 1929 (C089).
10. Letter, Edgar jr. to Liliane and Edgar Sr., May 3, 1930 (E008).
11. For information on Hammer, Paul Evans Holbrook, *An Introduction to Victor & Carolyn Hammer with a Listing of the Books Printed at their Several Presses* (Lexington, Kentucky: The Anvil Press, 1995).
12. Undated and unsigned typed manuscript, annotated in Edgar Kaufmann jr.'s handwriting as written by Hammer, filed with Kaufmann papers at Fallingwater (I-45).
13. Letter, Edgar jr. to Edgar Sr., June 8, 1931 (C091).
14. Letter, Liliane to Edgar Sr., March 22, 1931 (D013).
15. Letters, Edgar Sr. to Edgar jr., May 12, 1931 (C012a), and June 30, 1931 (C013a).
16. Letter, Edgar jr. to Edgar Sr., April 22, 1932 (C016a).
17. Letter, Edgar Sr. to Edgar jr., June 30, 1931 (C013a).
18. Letters, Edgar Sr. to Edgar jr., February 9, 1932 (C097), and Edgar jr. to Edgar Sr., April 7, 1932 (C043).
19. Letters, Edgar Sr. to Edgar jr., November 9, 1932 (C069a), and Edgar jr. to Liliane, undated, ca. 1933 [F119].
20. Letter, Edgar Sr. to Edgar jr., April 4, 1932 (C015).
21. Letter, Liliane to Edgar jr., undated [F226].
22. Letters, Liliane to Edgar jr., April 11, 1932 (F053), and April 29, [1932] [F272].
23. Letter, Edgar Sr. to Edgar jr., January 5, [1933] (C070a). Written early in the new year, his secretary

dated the letter 1932, but as it refers to the election of Roosevelt in November 1932, the year had to be 1933.
24. Letter, Edgar jr. to Liliane, undated (F116), and telegram, Edgar Sr. and Liliane to Edgar jr., July 25, 1933 (E054).
25. Letter, Edgar jr. to Edgar Sr., February 6, 1933 (C090).
26. Letter, Richard B. Freeman, Head, Department of Art, University of Kentucky, Lexington, to Edgar jr., July 20, 1961 [I-127]. An inventory of those works is filed with the Kaufmann papers at Fallingwater [I-59].
27. Letter, Edgar Sr. to Edgar jr., February 11, 1936 (C071). According to Kaufmann's letterhead, store representatives were maintained in Paris, Belfast, Berlin, Leipzig, Florence, Brussels, Vienna, and Istanbul.
28. Letter, Liliane to Edgar jr., March 11, 1933 [F222]. Earlier mentions of the shop and of her volunteer work at a hospital appear in letters, Liliane to Edgar jr., April 2 [1932] (F069), December 24/26 [1932] [F223], and December 31/January 2, 1932/1933 [F220].
29. Toker, 62, 350.
30. Edgar Kaufmann jr., *Fallingwater: A Frank Lloyd Wright Country House* (New York: Abbeville Press, 1986), 36.
31. Frank Lloyd Wright, *An Autobiography* (London, New York and Toronto: Longmans, Green and Company, 1932).
32. Donald Hoffmann, *Frank Lloyd Wright's Fallingwater: The House and Its History* (New York: Dover Publications, 1978), 11–12. Hoffmann's is one of several books that detail the background and building of Fallingwater as well as other Kaufmann commissions to Wright. Others include Richard L. Cleary, *Merchant Prince and Master Builder: Edgar J. Kaufmann and Frank Lloyd Wright* (Pittsburgh: The Heinz Architectural Center, Carnegie Museum of Art, in association with the University of Washington Press, 1999) as well as Franklin Toker's book noted below.
33. Franklin Toker, *Fallingwater Rising: Frank Lloyd Wright, E. J. Kaufmann, and America's Most Extraordinary House* (New York: Alfred A. Knopf, 2003).
34. Toker, 10, 120, 122, 368–69, 371.
35. Toker, 9, 444.
36. The organization was the New York Chapter of the Society of Architectural Historians, during which time, in 1975, Edgar jr. was president. Such use of the lower case *j* is not unique, yet continues to vex editors, who seem to have no problem with the spelling of the poet "e. e. cummings."
37. For example, letter, Purdy to Edgar jr., July 30, 1929 [G48].
38. Edna Offner to Purdy, October 23, 1934 (A003). At the time she had recently moved to Los Angeles, where she relates that she was working in the stenographic department at Universal Studios.
39. Edna Offner to Edgar jr., November 1, 1934 (A004).

40. Hoffmann, 11–12. This first visit is recorded by Marybud Lautner, "At Taliesin: September 27, 1934," in Randolph C. Henning, editor, *At Taliesin: Newspaper Columns by Frank Lloyd Wright and the Taliesin Fellowship, 1934–1937* (Carbondale: Southern Illinois University Press, 1992), 82.

41. Letter, Edgar Sr. to Edgar jr., October 20, 1934 (C017a).

42. Letter, Purdy to Edgar jr., undated [G002].

43. Letter, Edgar jr. to Liliane and Edgar Sr., undated (E038).

44. Letter, Edgar jr. to Liliane [October 1934] [F236].

45. The Kaufmanns' visit is recorded in Frank Lloyd Wright, "At Taliesin: November 22, 1934," Henning, 87. Liliane's letter to Edgar jr. is undated but makes clear reference to their recent visit (F032).

46. Hoffmann, 12–13. Both the planned December meeting and the funding of the model are further confirmed in a letter from Edgar Sr. to Edgar jr., December 5, 1934 (C019).

47. They left Taliesin on January 23, arriving in Chandler on January 29; Henning, 106.

48. Letter, Edgar jr. to Liliane, undated (F015).

49. Letter, Liliane to Edgar jr., March 8, 1935 (E024).

50. As related by Edgar Tafel and Robert Mosher in Edgar Tafel, *About Wright: An Album of Recollections by Those Who Knew Frank Lloyd Wright* (New York: John Wiley & Sons, 1993), 115, 148.

51. Cleary, 27.

52. Letter, Edgar Sr. to Edgar jr., April 12, 1935 (C004).

53. Letter, Bill Bernoudy to Edgar jr., April 24, 1935 (A020). William Adair (Bill) Bernoudy from St. Louis was a member of the fellowship from 1932 to 1935 and had worked on the Broadacre models; Henning, *At Taliesin*, 111, 309.

54. Information on some of the short-term apprentices is drawn from interviews over the years with Bruce Brooks Pfeiffer and Oscar Muñoz at Taliesin West.

55. As discussed in Brendan Gill, "Edgar Kaufmann, Jr.—Secrets of Wright and Fallingwater," *Architectural Digest* 47 (March 1990), 50–64, and Roger Friedland and Harold Zellman, *The Fellowship: The Untold Story of Frank Lloyd Wright & The Taliesin Fellowship* (New York: Harper Perennial, 2006), especially 271. Both accounts make clear that Edgar jr. was hardly the only homosexual at the fellowship; while such behavior was not generally encouraged, apparently it was at least tolerated.

56. Letter, Sim Richards to Edgar jr., May 26, 1935 (A019). Sim Bruce Richards, from Phoenix, was a member of the fellowship from May 1934 to September 1935; Henning, *At Taliesin*, 314.

57. Ibid.

58. Letter, Frank Lloyd Wright to Edgar Sr., December 11, 1950; filed with the Kaufmann papers (unnumbered folder), Drawings and Archives, Avery Architectural and Fine Arts Library, Columbia University in the City of New York (hereafter Avery Library).

59. For example, Christopher Wilk, *Frank Lloyd Wright: The Kaufmann Office* (London: The Victoria and Albert Museum, 1993), 51–52.

60. As reported in Hoffmann, 62, 66, 78.

61. Letter, Edgar Tafel to Edgar jr., March 25, 1939; letter, George E. Gillen of Gillen Woodwork Corporation to Edgar jr., August 16, 1937; Kaufmann papers, Avery Library.

62. Telegram, Frank Lloyd Wright to Edgar Sr., April 2, 1937; Kaufmann papers, Avery Library.

63. Edgar Kaufmann jr., *Fallingwater*, 172, and Hoffmann, 34.

64. Letter, Liliane to Edgar jr., August 5, 1935 (F023).

65. Letter, Liliane to Edgar jr., undated (F066).

66. Letter, Edgar jr. to Liliane, undated [F239]. Liliane's acceptance of Wright's design for her bedroom will be cited below.

67. Hoffmann, 69.

68. Telegram, Frank Lloyd Wright to John McAndrew, January 5, 1938. Registrar, Exhibition Files, Exh. #70. The Museum of Modern Art Archives, New York.

69. REG, Exh. #70, MoMA Archives, NY.

70. Hoffmann, 70.

71. His address was Apartment 7, Insurgentes 70; letter, Edgar Sr. to Edgar jr., July 31, 1941 (C081); he enclosed a sketch of its layout in an undated letter to his mother (E015).

72. Letters, Liliane to Edgar jr., May 6, 1941 [F166], and Edgar Sr. to Edgar jr., May 16, 1941 (C077).

73. Letters, Edgar Sr. to Edgar jr., April 18, 1941 (C076), and July 24, 1941 (C079). Toker reports that they left La Torelle in 1940 and rented an apartment at the William Penn Hotel in downtown Pittsburgh; Toker, 308. In a letter from Edgar jr. to his parents, March 13, 1944, the address is listed as 1566 William Penn Hotel (E022).

74. Letters, Edgar Sr. to Edgar jr., May 25, 1943 (C025) and October 8, 1943 (C031).

75. He enlisted on September 17, 1942, and left service on November 30, 1945, according to the official Military Record and Report of Separation filed with the Kaufmann family letters at Fallingwater (A002).

76. Letter, Edgar jr. to Liliane, June 15 (year not given) [F242].

77. Letters, Aline Bernstein Louchheim to Edgar jr., August 5, 1943 (B032) and September 24 (year not given) (B040).

78. Toker, 216, 393, 461.

79. The two diaries were among Kaufmann documents given to me by Aldo Radoczy; I have since given them to the National Library of Australia, Canberra, so that they might be reunited with the others in their archive.

80. As recorded by Friend on August 20, 1946. I am grateful for this and following references to Ian Britain, who in May 2010 compiled "References to and letters from Edgar J. Kaufmann jr. in the diaries of Donald Friend, held at the National Library of Australia, Canberra." As he recounts, some but not all of the entries are published in the National Library's edition of the diaries, 4 vols. (Canberra, 2001–06).

81. Cleary, 81, note 26. Documents that would have confirmed Kaufmann's duties at the museum were not available in the Museum of Modern Art Archive when I was there in May 2010.

82. Letter, Liliane to Edgar jr., February 10 [1946?] [F146].

83. Letter, Liliane to Edgar jr., March 19 [1951] [F139].

84. Letter, Liliane to Frank Lloyd Wright, March 19 [1951], Folder 1, Box 1, filed with the Kaufmann papers, Avery Library. For further discussion of this, Toker, 347–48.

85. Letters, Liliane to Frank Lloyd Wright, undated, Folder 1, Box 1, Kaufmann papers, Avery Library; and Liliane to Edgar jr., April 4, 1951 [F140].

86. Anthony Alofsin, editor, *Frank Lloyd Wright: An Index to the Taliesin Correspondence*, 5 vols. (New York: Garland, 1988).

87. Letter, Liliane to Edgar jr., March 29 [1951] [F137].

88. Typed manuscript in Fallingwater archive. The exhibition ran from November 12, 1940, to January 5, 1941, but the catalogue was not published, as explained in a later publication of the material: Peter Reed and William Kaizen, editors, *The Show to End All Shows: Frank Lloyd Wright and the Museum of Modern Art, 1940* (New York: The Museum of Modern Art, 2004). All three Kaufmanns submitted pieces, and all are reproduced there: Edgar Sr., 170–79; Liliane, 180–81; and Edgar jr., 181–84.

89. A telegram from Olgivanna Lloyd Wright to Edgar jr., September 7, 1952 (A060) confirms this date.

90. Letter, Edgar jr. to Paul Mayén, postmarked April 15, 1955. The letter is among papers given to me by Aldo Radoczy but will be given to Fallingwater.

91. "Edgar J. Kaufmann jr.: Publications 1938–1989," compiled by Alfred Willis in Edgar Kaufmann jr., *9 Commentaries on Frank Lloyd Wright* (New York and Cambridge, Mass: The Architectural History Foundation and the MIT Press, 1989), 137–56. Kaufmann taught at Columbia University from 1964 to 1980.

92. Kaufmann, *Fallingwater*, 59–60.

93. Letter, Barbara L. Zinsser; Polier, Midonick & Zinsser, Attorneys and Counselors at Law, New York City, to Edgar jr., September 11, 1959; among Kaufmann papers in my possession, to be given to Fallingwater.

94. Letter, Olgivanna Lloyd Wright to Edgar jr., March 8, 1984 (A070).

95. Typed manuscript, "Remarks on Fallingwater," March 1985, Edgar Kaufmann jr. The manuscript is among papers in my possession and will be given to Fallingwater.

To Hear Fallingwater Is to See It in Time by Neil Levine

1. In "Frank Lloyd Wright," *Architectural Forum* 68 (January 1938): 36.
2. Philip Johnson, "Whence and Whither: The Processional Element in Architecture," orig. pub. *Perspecta* 9/10 (1965), repr. in Johnson, *Writings* (New York: Oxford University Press, 1979), 151–55. For an earlier iteration of this idea, specifically in relation to Wright's architecture, see Johnson, "100 Years, Frank Lloyd Wright and Us," orig. pub. *Pacific Architect and Builder* (March 1957), repr. in Johnson, *Writings*, 196–98.
3. John McAndrew, *A New House by Frank Lloyd Wright on Bear Run, Pennsylvania* (New York: Museum of Modern Art, January 1938). The Wright text along with several of the same photographs were published contemporaneously in "Wright," *Architectural Forum*, 36–47.
4. Because the interior furnishings had not yet been completed, only a view of the study area was included. It was enlivened by books on the shelves, writing accoutrements on the desk, and plantings behind.
5. To be absolutely precise, it should be noted that the nighttime shot zooms in slightly more than the daytime one.
6. In McAndrew, *New House*, n.p.
7. For information on the visit and the family's use of the property, see Donald Hoffmann, *Frank Lloyd Wright's Fallingwater: The House and Its History*, 2nd rev. ed. (New York: Dover, 1993), 15–16, 34; and Edgar Kaufmann jr., "Frank Lloyd Wright's Fallingwater 25 Years After," *Architettura* 8 (August 1962): 255. Kaufmann jr.'s later *Fallingwater: A Frank Lloyd Wright Country House* (New York: Abbeville Press, 1986), esp. 31, 36, 124, reconstructs the events differently and much less convincingly in my view. See my *The Architecture of Frank Lloyd Wright* (Princeton, N.J.: Princeton University Press, 1996), 227–34.
8. Frank Lloyd Wright to Edgar Kaufmann, 26 December 1934, in *Frank Lloyd Wright: Letters to Clients*, ed. Bruce Brooks Pfeiffer (Fresno: Press at California State University, 1986), 82.
9. In his review of the recently completed structure, Lewis Mumford, "The Sky Line—at Home, Indoors and Out," *The New Yorker* 13 (12 February 1938): 31, wrote: "The stones represent, as it were, the earth theme; the concrete slabs are the water theme."
10. Quoted in Edgar Tafel, *Apprentice to Genius: Years with Frank Lloyd Wright* (New York: McGraw-Hill, 1979), 7.
11. Two interlocking semicircular forms were employed to give the walkway connecting the guest house to the main house a cascading effect when the former structure was built in 1938–39.
12. Wright to Kaufmann, 2 April 1937, Box ST 22, Avery Library, Columbia University, New York.
13. Although there is no reason whatsoever to believe that Wright had them in mind, many ancient Roman floor mosaics were designed to imitate the effect of moving water. The tradition persisted throughout the Byzantine and early medieval periods in the Mediterranean, the most spectacular example being the book-matched marble floors of Hagia Sophia in Istanbul. See Fabio Barry, "Walking on Water: Cosmic Floors in Antiquity and the Middle Ages," *Art Bulletin* 89 (December 2007): 627–56.
14. Wright reused the idea of a curved resonating chamber to transmit the sound of water in the oceanfront project for the Morris House, outside San Francisco (1944–46). There, a well leading down through the base of the house to an opening along the shore would have carried the sound of the lapping waves to the upper living floors.
15. Frank Lloyd Wright, *An Autobiography* (London, New York, and Toronto: Longmans, Green, 1932), 173.
16. Yukio Futagawa and Paul Rudolph, *Global Architecture*, vol. 2, *Frank Lloyd Wright: Kaufmann House, "Fallingwater," Bear Run, Pennsylvania, 1936* (Tokyo: A.D.A. EDITA, 1970), n.p.

Fallingwater's Interiors: Rustic Elegance and Flexible Living by Justin Gunther

1. Wright based the ocher for the concrete in what he called the key "of the sere leaves of the rhododendron." Fallingwater's Cherokee red was based on a Native American pot in Wright's collection and evoked the properties inherent in the steel. See Donald Hoffmann, *Frank Lloyd Wright's Fallingwater: The House and Its History*, 2nd rev. ed. (New York: Dover Publications, Inc., 1993), 61–65. For Liliane's remarks on the color scheme, see her untitled essay reprinted in Peter Reed and William Kaizen, editors, *The Show to End All Shows: Frank Lloyd Wright and the Museum of Modern Art, 1940* (New York: Museum of Modern Art, 2004), 180–81.
2. Frederick Gutheim, ed., *Frank Lloyd Wright on Architecture; Selected Writings, 1894–1940* (New York: Duell, Sloan, and Pearce, 1941), 236.
3. Edgar Kaufmann jr., introduction to Hoffmann, vii.
4. Fallingwater retains 169 pieces of site-specific furniture designed by Wright, representing one of the most complete ensembles still with its original house. Gillen Woodworking Corporation, previously the Matthews Company, was formed by George E. Gillen in 1937 after Matthews was sold at auction and reorganized. Gillen was also responsible for the millwork in Wright's Darwin Martin House and Wingspread. For a thorough study of Gillen Woodworking, see Franklin Toker, *Fallingwater Rising: Frank Lloyd Wright, E. J. Kaufmann, and America's Most Extraordinary House* (New York: Alfred A. Knopf, 2004), 237–41. For Wright's opinions on wood, see Frank Lloyd Wright, "In the Cause of Architecture: The Meaning of Materials—Wood," *Architectural Record* 63 (May 1928): 481.
5. The terms *zabuton* and *hassock* were specified by Wright. A zabuton is a Japanese floor cushion. The term *hassock* has an Old English derivation and is a synonym for ottoman. Dunlopillo was manufactured by the Dunlop Tire & Rubber Company of Buffalo, New York. The product was originally introduced for more public buildings, such as churches, hospitals, and theaters. See Hoffmann, 70.
6. Edgar Kaufmann jr.'s discussion of movable furniture can be found in an unpublished document in the Fallingwater Archives entitled "Edited Text of Fallingwater Discussion, 31 May 1974."
7. Numerous layout drawings drafted at Taliesin during the planning of Fallingwater document these proposals. Located in the archives of the Frank Lloyd Wright Foundation, drawings of particular note are 3602.078, 3602.52, and 3602.141. The prototype for the barrel chair survives at Fallingwater and is on display in the guest house bedroom. Actual patterns for rugs are unknown. Kaufmann jr. discusses his family's rejection of these proposals in his untitled

essay for MoMA's 1940 exhibition *Frank Lloyd Wright: American Architect*, reprinted in Reed and Kaizen, 181–84. The three-legged chairs were purchased at a Florentine antique shop in the Via dei Fossi owned by Coppini; see Liliane Kaufmann, letter to Edgar Kaufmann jr., no date, Kaufmann Correspondence Collection, F186; Fallingwater Archives (Mill Run, PA).

8. The first commercial fluorescent lamps were made by General Electric and came onto the market in 1938. After seeing fluorescents exhibited at the 1939 New York World's Fair, Kaufmann jr. recommended them for Fallingwater. See Kaufmann jr., *Fallingwater: A Frank Lloyd Wright Country House* (New York: Abbeville Press, 1986), 121. Originally, Japanese rice paper was planned for the ceiling light screens. Unbleached muslin was used instead, per the recommendation of Kaufmann jr.; Edgar Kaufmann jr., letter to Liliane Kaufmann, 27 May 1943, Kaufmann Correspondence Collection, F043; Fallingwater Archives (Mill Run, PA).

9. Kaufmann jr., *Fallingwater: A Frank Lloyd Wright Country House*, 131.

10. Information on individual collection items is pulled from object files in the Fallingwater Archives. The Hangover was a pre-cut cabin ordered from the Aladdin Company of Bay City, Michigan; bill of sale in the Fallingwater Archives. For more on La Torelle, see Donald Miller, *The Architecture of Benno Janssen* (Pittsburgh: Carnegie Mellon University, 1997), 79–91. In previously published scholarship, the spelling of the house is with a "u": La Tourelle. The Kaufmanns never used this spelling, evidenced by their letterhead for the house and personal correspondence. For more on Samuel Yellin, see Jack Andrews, *Samuel Yellin, Metalworker* (Ocean Pines, MD: Skipjack Press, 2000). The reference to the purchase of the Madonna and Child sculpture from French & Company can be found in an unpublished document entitled "Fallingwater Fact Sheet" created c.1970 under the guidance of Edgar Kaufmann jr. for the purposes of guide training.

11. For a summary of the 1930 Kaufmann's department store remodel see Richard L. Cleary, *Merchant Prince and Master Builder: Edgar J. Kaufmann and Frank Lloyd Wright*, exh. cat. (Pittsburgh: The Heinz Architectural Center, Carnegie Museum of Art/Seattle and London: University of Washington Press, 1999), 22–26. Kaufmann's speech was published in the special "Kaufmann's Supplement" of the *Pittsburgh Sun–Telegraph*, Sunday, 11 May 1930. For more on the murals, see Albert Christ-Janer, *Boardman Robinson* (Chicago: University of Chicago Press, 1946); *Boardman Robinson: American Muralist & Illustrator, 1876–1952*, exh. cat. (Colorado Springs: Colorado Springs Fine Arts Center, 1996).

12. See Cleary, 26. The development of the Vendôme shops can also be traced through the Kaufmann Correspondence Collection in the Fallingwater Archives.

13. Franklin Toker analyzes the ethnic and national origins of the collection in *Fallingwater Rising*. See Toker, 311.

14. Milk glass is predominantly located in the master bedroom bathroom. Liliane purchased farm chairs for the kitchen's work table, which was designed by Wright. The salt-glazed stoneware in the Kaufmanns' collection was primarily made by western Pennsylvania potteries in Fayette and Greene counties, and stoneware on display today is a fraction of the original collection.

15. W. Frank Purdy served as Kaufmann jr.'s mentor throughout his childhood, and this connection is documented in the Kaufmann Correspondence Collection. Before directing the Ferargil Galleries, Purdy served as director of the School of American Sculpture and head of Gorham's sculpture department; see *The American Magazine of Art*, Vol. 13, No. 11 (Nov. 1922).

16. The bust of W. Frank Purdy was exhibited at the Arden Galleries in 1939; see *Parnassus*, Vol. 11, No. 3 (March 1939): 33. Correspondence related to the commission of the Purdy bust can be found in letter G026 of the Kaufmann Correspondence Collection. For placement of the McClendon statue, see letter E030 written on 20 Dec. 1943 from Edgar Kaufmann jr. to his parents. For more on Rose McClendon and Richmond Barthé, see Margaret Rose Vendryes, *Barthé: A Life in Sculpture* (Jackson: University Press of Mississippi, 2008), 31.

17. Images of Gábor's displays at Kaufmann's can be found in Emrich Nicholson, *Contemporary Shops in the United States* (New York: Architectural Books Publishing Co., Inc., 1945), 148–53. Gábor's immigration is documented in letter F022, 1 Feb. 1935. Kaufmann jr.'s introduction to Gábor can be found in letter G030. Various V-mails and letters in the Kaufmann Correspondence Collection further reveal the family's relationship with Gábor.

18. For a discussion on Josef Frank and Kaufmann's department store, see Christopher Long, *Josef Frank: Life and Work* (Chicago: The University of Chicago Press, 2002), 234–35.

19. When exhibited at the Carnegie International in 1930, *Excursion* won best in show; see *Twenty-ninth Annual International Exhibition of Paintings, October 16–December 7, 1930*, exh. cat. (Pittsburgh: Carnegie Institute, 1930). A description of the Stamperia del Santuccio can be found in a small pamphlet, Joseph Graves, *Victor Hammer: Calligrapher, Punch-cutter & Printer* (Charlottesville: Bibliographical Society of the University of Virginia, 1954). As documented in the Kaufmann Correspondence Collection, during Kaufmann jr.'s apprenticeship, the family provided significant financial support for the workshop in return for artwork, making the Kaufmanns one of the great patrons of the artist's career. The printing of *Samson Agonistes* was the first book produced by Hammer's workshop. The Kaufmanns were integral in securing Philadephia's A.S.W. Rosenbach as the distributor, and Kaufmann jr. wrote the prospectus. Paul Koch's gift of music printing is documented in letter C097, dated 9 Feb. 1932. The Bach Menuett on display in Fallingwater is one of a limited edition of 150 printed on the hand press of the Officina Vindobonensis in Vienna, published at Georg Kallmeyer in Wolfenbüttel; see unpublished article by Warren Chappell in the Fallingwater Archives.

20. For a discussion of exhibitions held at Kaufmann's, see Cleary, 28–34. Photographs of *Below the Rio Grande* survive in the Fallingwater Archives.

21. Liliane Kaufmann, letter to Edgar Kaufmann jr., no date, Kaufmann Correspondence Collection, F065.

22. Liliane Kaufmann recounts her introduction to Diego Rivera and Frida Kahlo on a trip to Mexico with Kaufmann jr., in letter D019, 17 May 1938, Kaufmann Correspondence Collection. Kaufmann jr. traveled extensively in Mexico with MoMA's John McAndrew during the summer of 1941, likely as part of the museum's buying trips in Latin America and Cuba; see letters E012-014. The Kaufmanns' introduction to Magaña is documented in letters C078, 3 July 1941, and C079, 24 July 1941. For more on the sculptor, see Juan Coronel, et al., *El Sentir de la Tradición: Mardonio Magaña* (Mexico, D.F.: Editorial RM, 2003). For MoMA's 1943 exhibition, the Kaufmanns were credited with providing purchase funds, and their Velasco, *Landscape: Jalapa, Mexico*, was featured; see Lincoln Kirstein, *The Latin-American Collection of the Museum of Modern Art*, exh. cat. (New York: Museum of Modern Art, 1943), 19. Liliane's interest in *recuerdas* is documented in letter D017, dated 10 May 1938.

23. Edgar Kaufmann jr., *What is Modern Design?* exh. cat. (New York: Museum of Modern Art, 1950).

24. The Kaufmanns' extensive collection of Tiffany was largely purchased through New York's Lillian Nassau. The structural comparison of the Tiffany lampshade was made in Kaufmann, *Fallingwater: A Frank Lloyd Wright Country House*, 136.

25. See unpublished document in Fallingwater Archives, "Edgar J. Kaufmann jr. Tour of Fallingwater, April 1985," 20.

26. Kaufmann jr. played a significant role in the acceptance of Mathsson in the United States; see Dag Widman, Karin Winter, and Nina Stritzler-Levine, *Bruno Mathsson* (Malmö and Stockholm: Bokförlaget Arena/New York: Bard Graduate Center for Studies in the Decorative Arts, Design and Culture/New Haven: Yale University Press, 2006). Kaufmann jr. introduced Finn Juhl to the United States through a Nov. 1948, v. 108, 96–99 article published in

Contract Interiors, "Finn Juhl of Copenhagen." He also maintained a long-term friendship with the designer, as evidenced in the Kaufmann Correspondence Collection. For more, see Esbjorn Hiort, *Finn Juhl: Furniture, Architecture, Applied Art* (Copenhagen: The Danish Architectural Press, 1990).

27. For more on Speyer, see *A. James Speyer: Architect, Curator, Exhibition Designer*, exh. cat. (Chicago: The Art Club of Chicago/Pittsburgh: Carnegie Museum of Art, The Heinz Architectural Center/Athens: National Technical University of Athens, School of Architecture, 1997).

28. For more on Tillie Speyer, see *Three Decades of Sculpture by Tillie Speyer*, exh. cat. (Pittsburgh: Museum of Art, Carnegie Institute, 1978). Sideo Fromboluti and his art are discussed in detail in *Sideo Fromboluti: Summer Painting*, exh. cat. (Provincetown: Provincetown Art Association and Museum/Paris: Galeria Darthea Speyer/Pittsburgh: The Forum Gallery, Carnegie Museum of Art, 1998).

29. Edgar Kaufmann jr., "Frank Lloyd Wright and the Fine Arts," *Perspecta* 8 (1963): 42.

30. Ibid.; also see Kaufmann jr., *Fallingwater: A Frank Lloyd Wright Country House*, 131. Included in the collection at Fallingwater are tomb panels from the Sung dynasty, wall-mounted Chinese figures of an unknown date, a bronze head of Buddha, a statue of Goddess Parvati from c.750 AD, and a Ming dynasty teapot.

31. A Zuni Pueblo pot is prominently displayed in the living room. Two San Ildefonso Pueblo pots by Maria Martinez are displayed in Edgar Kaufmann jr.'s study. For more on Maria Martinez, see Richard Spivey, *The Legacy of Maria Poveka Martinez* (Santa Fe: Museum of New Mexico Press, 2003). A letter documenting the purchase of Modoc Indian baskets in California was written by Liliane, F104, no date, Kaufmann Correspondence Collection. The Kaufmanns spent much time in Southern California, eventually building a house designed by Richard Neutra in Palm Springs.

32. Information regarding objects removed was derived from three sources in the Fallingwater Archives: "Fallingwater Work Schedules and Inventory, 1957," "Reed, Smith, Shaw & McClay: Recorded Capital Investment of Mr. Edgar J. Kaufmann in Residential Portion of his Bear Run Property at April 15, 1955," and "Works of Art Owned by Professor Edgar J. Kaufmann Jr.," compiled by Franklin Toker and Rebecca Maclean, 6 April 1999. Rodin's *Iris* is pictured in Bruno Zevi and Edgar Kaufmann jr., *La Casa sulla Cascata di F. Ll. Wright, Frank Lloyd Wright's Fallingwater*, 2nd ed. (Milan, Italy: ETAS Kompass, March 1965), and was sold in 1989 through Sotheby's. See *Modern Paintings and Sculpture from the Collection of the late Edgar J. Kaufmann, Jr.*, auction catalogue (New York: Sotheby's, 1989).

33. The Picasso aquatints displayed in Fallingwater are *The Artist and His Model*, 1963, and *The Smoker*, 1964. For more on Lyonel Feininger's *Church on the Cliffs* series see William S. Lieberman, ed., *Lyonel Feininger: The Ruin by the Sea* (New York: Museum of Modern Art, 1968). The Bryan Hunt commission is documented in *Bryan Hunt: Twenty Years, October 6–November 11, 1995*, exh. cat. (Philadelphia: Locks Gallery, 1995). Images of the Marini survive in the Fallingwater Archives and were published in Zevi. Only fragments of the sculpture were recovered after the 1956 flood.

34. For Kaufmann jr.'s opinions on textiles, see Kaufmann jr., *Fallingwater: A Frank Lloyd Wright Country House*, 131; unpublished "Edgar J. Kaufmann jr. Tour of Fallingwater, April 1985." Jack Lenor Larsen recounts his friendship with Kaufmann jr. in *Jack Lenor Larsen: A Weaver's Memoir* (New York: H. N. Abrams, 1998).

35. Kaufmann jr. documented his desire for flexibility in "Toward a Fulfillment of Fallingwater," an unpublished document in the Fallingwater Archives dated 8 May 1986.

Fallingwater: Integrated Architecture's Modern Legacy and Sustainable Prospect by John M. Reynolds

1. Howett, Catherine. "Modernism and American Landscape Architecture." In *Modern Landscape Architecture: A Critical Review* (Cambridge: The MIT Press, 1993), 21.

2. Cole, Thomas. "Essay on American Scenery," *The American Monthly Magazine* New Series 1 (January 1836): 9–10.

3. Please see "Florilegia Naturalis: The Aesthetic, Scientific and Ethical Valorization of Nature" in: Porphyrios, Demetri. *Sources of Modern Eclecticism* (London: Academy Editions, 1982), 59–81.

4. Heidegger, Martin. *Poetry, Language, Thought*. trans. Albert Hofstadler *(*New York: Harper and Row, 1975), 147.

5. Harries, Karsten. "Cultivate." Unpublished Essay, Yale University, New Haven, Connecticut, 2007. 1–2.

6. Curtis, William J. R., *Le Corbusier: Ideas and Forms* (New York: Rizzoli, 1986), 96–97.

7. Ibid. 96.

8. Mies van der Rohe, in an interview with Christian Norberg-Schulz, cited in Howett, Catherine. "Modernism and American Landscape Architecture." In *Modern Landscape Architecture: A Critical Review* (Cambridge: The MIT Press, 1993), 27.

9. Porphyrios, Demetri. *Sources of Modern Eclecticism* (London: Academy Editions, 1982), 2.

10. Ibid. 1.

11. Ibid. 2.

12. Weston, Richard. *Alvar Aalto* (London: Phaidon Press Limited, 1995), 81.

13. Holl, Steven. *Intertwining* (New York: Princeton Architectural Press, 1996), 15.

14. Robert McCarter in *Fallingwater: Frank Lloyd Wright* cites the photographs of Henry Hamilton Bennett and the observations of Thomas Beeby as found in: Beeby, Thomas. "Wright and Landscape: A Mythical Interpretation." In *The Nature of Frank Lloyd Wright* (Chicago: The University of Chicago Press, 1988), 154–72.

15. Wright, Frank Lloyd. *The Future of Architecture* (New York: Bramhill House, 1953), 321–22.

16. Ibid.

17. Ibid.

18. Frampton, Kenneth. *Modern Architecture: A Critical History* (New York: Thames & Hudson, 1992), 189.

19. McCarter, Robert. *Fallingwater: Frank Lloyd Wright* (London: Phaidon Press Limited, 1994), 22.

20. Wright, Frank Lloyd. *The Living City* (New York: Horizon Press, 1958), 96.

21. Ibid. 97.

22. Ibid.

23. Ibid.

24. Ibid. 123.

25. Howett, Catherine. "Modernism and American

Landscape Architecture." In *Modern Landscape Architecture: A Critical Review* (Cambridge: The MIT Press, 1993), 25.

26. Bohlin, Peter. Interview by the author. Miami University, Oxford, Ohio. April 2007.

27. Leopold, Aldo. *A Sand County Almanac and Sketches Here and There.* (New York: Oxford University Press, 1982), viii.

28. Whitman, Walt. *Leaves of Grass: Comprehensive Reader's Edition.* Harold W. Blodgett & Sculley Bradley, eds. (New York: New York University Press, 1965).

29. Hoffmann, Donald. *Frankl Lloyd Wright's Fallingwater: The House and Its History.* (New York: Dover Publications, Inc., 1993), 110.

Appendix: Kaufmann Essays

1. Laszlo Gabor was a Hungarian painter and designer, formerly resident in Vienna, where he was the business director of the Österreichische Werkbund. The Kaufmann family had helped him to immigrate to the United States in 1935, and employed him in their department store.

Index

Acknowledgments

This book marks the 75th Anniversary of Fallingwater. In creating it we sought the assistance of many of those who have been closely associated with the site over the years. Without their help and encouragement, this project could not have been undertaken. I hope we have produced a book that will provide a fresh look at this great place and add significantly to our understanding of it.

Deep appreciation goes first to the Colcom Foundation of Pittsburgh. Their grant enabled us to travel for research and meetings and to undertake a much more ambitious book than would have otherwise been possible.

Special thanks is due the essayists. Each of these scholars knows Fallingwater intimately and willingly agreed to reexamine it sharing his insights into its history, architecture, collections, landscape, preservation, and legacy.

I was delighted that Christopher Little, our principal photographer, who first photographed the house for a publication that marked Fallingwater's 50th Anniversary in 1986, agreed to return. Over a yearlong period, he waded through rushing water, battled a legendary snowfall and climbed over boulders and through thickets of rhododendron to capture the subtleties and drama of this most photogenic of places. Working around thousands of visitors, he was meticulous in pursuing images that speak to Fallingwater's singular beauty.

Many individuals and institutions assisted the essayists in their research and granted permission to use images and materials from their collections. First, all of us owe a great debt of gratitude to Aldo Radoczy for his generous donation of a major collection of Kaufmann family correspondence, which made David De Long's article possible. At the Drawings and Archives collection at the Avery Architectural and Fine Arts Library, Columbia University, Janet Parks and Jason Escalante. At the Museum of Modern Art, New York, Peter Reed, Michele Elligott, and Jonathan Lill. At the Frank Lloyd Wright Archives, Taliesin West, Bruce Brooks Pfeiffer, Margo Stipe, and Oscar Muñoz. At the National Library of Australia, Canberra, Jan Fullerton and Maureen Brooks. Also in Australia, Ian Britian, editor of The Donald Friend Diaries. At the University of Pennsylvania, Suzanne Hyndman and Cara Bertron. At Robert Silman Associates, John Mateo.

At Fallingwater, Justin Gunther and Clinton Piper were invaluable members of our team.

Justin Gunther not only contributed an astute essay on the collections but also assisted many of the other authors with photographs, research, and archival materials. Clinton Piper assisted the authors and photographer in securing archival materials and served as sounding board and troubleshooter for the many challenges that arose in the course of the project. Thanks also to Tom Schmidt, Fallingwater's first director, for his support. At the Western Pennsylvania Conservancy's headquarters in Pittsburgh my thanks to Tom Saunders and Genny McIntyre for their confidence and encouragement.

To the members of the Fallingwater Advisory Committee I owe my sincere thanks for their enthusiastic support of this project, especially Michael Strueber, who encouraged us to seek funding from the Colcom Foundation, and David De Long, who contributed an essay.

Last, my heartfelt thanks to my husband, Tom, who provided encouragement, thoughtful advice and matchless proofreading skills. This book would not have been possible without his personal support.

—L.W.

Photographer's Note

When Lynda Waggoner asked me to re-photograph Mr. Wright's masterpiece, I was thrilled. It had been twenty-five years since I worked with Edgar Kaufmann jr. on *Fallingwater—A Frank Lloyd Wright Country House*. So I thank Lynda for the opportunity, for her friendship, and for the farsightedness with which she leads Fallingwater today. Thanks, too, go to Clinton Piper, Museum Programs Assistant, and to Curator Justin Gunther, who gracefully allowed himself to be pressed into service as my occasional assistant. Linda Henry, Dale Etta Matlick, and Nancy King clean Fallingwater, and I inconvenienced them daily. Same with the security team: Jerry Burke, Marla Bates, Glenn Johnson, Butch Hilliard, and the ever-patient interpretative guides, who welcomed me and often introduced me to their visitors. Finally, the indefatigable Albert Ohler takes care of everything, including photographers.

The stellar publishing team of Douglas Curran, David Morton, and the visionary Charles Miers were incredibly supportive of my efforts, and I owe them commensurate gratitude.

It was a great privilege to photograph Fallingwater again and to have the run of the house. I photographed in Winter, Spring, Summer, and Fall. Never once did I tire of the experience. There were always unexpected nuances and new images to discover. I encourage everyone to visit this national treasure. It is a work of art.

—C. L.